Praise for *A Long and Terrible Shadow*:

"Wonderfully done and argued, and very important."
—Peter Gzowski, *The Globe and Mail*

"A concise but surprisingly comprehensive survey of centuries of struggle, pain, and loss. . . . *A Long and Terrible Shadow*, like much of Thomas Berger's work, is likely to cast a shadow of its own, far into the future."
—Justin E. A. Busch, *Kingston Whig-Standard*

"One of those lucid summaries of an immensely complex topic that can only be written by people sure of who they are and what they know. . . . A profoundly intelligent and thoughtful study."
—Brian Fawcett, *Books in Canada*

"A broad and sobering examination of the European subjugation of native American peoples."
—Wayne Grady, *Equinox*

"*A Long and Terrible Shadow* is nothing less than optimistic, challenging the reader to embrace a new age of discovery, 'the second discovery of America,' and to see the 500th anniversary of Europe's arrival in the Americas as a triumph of the aboriginal peoples' will to survive."
—Terry Glavin, *Vancouver Sun*

"Berger's well-reasoned and lucid book confronts our European-bred rationalizations and ideological distortions of history. . . . Concise, scholarly, yet immensely readable."
—Daniel Ray, *Edmonton Journal*

"If you read only one serious work of non-fiction this year, it should be Thomas Berger's remarkable essay."
—Gerald Caplan, *Toronto Star*

A Long and Terrible Shadow

WHITE VALUES, NATIVE RIGHTS IN THE AMERICAS

1492–1992

Thomas R. Berger

DOUGLAS & McINTYRE
Vancouver/Toronto

UNIVERSITY OF WASHINGTON PRESS
Seattle

DOUGLAS & McINTYRE LTD.
1615 Venables Street
Vancouver, British Columbia V5L 2H1

Published simultaneously in the United States of America by the University of Washington Press, P.O. Box 50096, Seattle, WA 98145-5096

Canadian Cataloguing in Publication Data

Berger, Thomas R.
  A long and terrible shadow

  Includes bibliographical references and index.
  ISBN 1-55054-057-2

  1. Indigenous peoples—America.   2. Indians,
Treatment of.   3. Indians—Land tenure.   I. Title.
E98.L3B47 1991   323.1'197   C91-091622-5

Library of Congress Cataloging-in-Publication Data

Berger, Thomas R.
    A long and terrible shadow : white values, native rights in the Americas,
  1492–1992 / Thomas R. Berger.—1st paperback ed.
      p.   cm.
    Published simultaneously: Vancouver : Douglas & McIntyre, 1991.
    Includes bibliographical references and index.
    ISBN 0-295-97222-X (paper)
    1. Indians, Treatment of.   2. Indians—Land tenure.   3. Indians—
Politics and government.   I. Title.
E91.B47   1992   92-14370
323.1'197—dc20   CIP

Editing by Brian Scrivener
Design by The Typeworks
Cover design by Alexandra Hass
Cover image: Portion of P. Forlani and F. Bertelli's world map, *Universale
  Descrittione di Tutta La Terra* . . . , published in Venice, 1565. Courtesy of the
  National Archives of Canada, NMC 13294
Typeset by The Typeworks
Printed and bound in Canada by D. W. Friesen and Sons
Printed on acid-free paper ∞

Contents

Acknowledgments

When I undertook to write this book, I was able to enlist Drew Ann Wake as my part-time research assistant. Her knowledge of Latin America and her access to materials in Spanish and Portuguese made it possible for me to discuss the history of times and places not well known to North Americans. She also helped me in working out the shape and structure of the book. Val Chapman, my secretary for many years, allowed the project to pursue her into retirement; she typed draft after draft with her usual patience and competence. My editor, Brian Scrivener, greatly improved the book. Scott McIntyre encouraged me all along, insisting that having set my hand to the plow I should complete the furrow. I am sure he was right. My other books about Native people and Native rights were the product of inquiries into specific issues. My object was to enable

Native people to speak for themselves. This book is my opportunity
to speak for myself.

Vancouver, British Columbia
17 June 1991

Introduction

In December 1990 I stood amid the stones of Macchu Picchu, the lost city of the Incas. An engineering marvel, it inspires wonder and amazement. Poet Pablo Neruda called it "Tall city of stepped stone." We can only speculate at the organization, the skill and the dedication required to build such a city high in the Andes, so inaccessible that four hundred years passed before its existence became known to us.

What of the people who built it? Where are they now? Well, they are still here, at the railway station below, at the beginning of the ascent, selling weavings and sweaters to tourists. These people—descendants of the Incas and their subject tribes—number in the millions, here in the Andean highlands. Are they nothing more than a forlorn remnant of a civilization that ceased to exist long ago, living today on the periphery of the dominant European society? Are they simply the flesh and blood counterpart of the ruins of Macchu Picchu, a reminder of what once was, but no longer exists in any sense that is important to us?

Spain conquered the empire of the Incas, bringing war, disease and famine. The Spanish, like the other Europeans who followed them to the New World, assumed that they had the right to another people's lands, the right to their labour, the right even to take from them the legitimacy of their own past. For the early European colonists, the Indians were alien and primitive, of uncertain humanity, arguably without rights. Although five hundred years have passed, the moral and intellectual distance between those of us of European descent and Native peoples often seems as great as ever.

When the Europeans came to the New World in 1492 it was to bring to the Indians the true Christ and the blessings of civilization. The Indians were enjoined to reject their own religion, their own way of life, their own past. Today we bring a similar faith, but it is a faith in ourselves, in our technology, and in the way of life of the dominant society. The ideas we live by and the institutions that govern us are European in origin. The built environment is ours. The place of the Indians in this world is indistinct and shadowy. In South America what remains of pre-Columbian civilizations consists of ruins such as Macchu Picchu and, in the streets of Andean cities, diminutive Indian women in bowler hats, nursing their babies, selling handicrafts, and begging. Nor is it any different in North America. In Canada and the United States when we think of Indians we imagine dilapidated Indian reserves and reservations, or Indians, drunk and dishevelled, on the skid rows of our cities.

Today, as in 1492, we profess to bring to the Indians modernity, release from a primitive way of life and, most important of all, the idea of the autonomy of the individual. Set against these, what contribution have the Indians made to the history of the New World? How can a case be made for measures to protect what is left of Indian society? Is this how their story should end—by the dissolution of Indian collectivities and their absorption in the dominant society, no longer clinging to their crafts and carvings, a last sad celebration of memories and myths?

Since 1492, Native institutions, their lifeways and their lands have been under attack. The history of the Americas has been the history of the encroachment of European societies on the Native peoples. The imposition of European values on Native communities has entailed an attempt to inculcate European ideas of development, of economic progress, of the paramountcy of saving, accumulation and investment. Columbus, writing to the king and queen of Spain, described the Indians of the West Indies as, "So tractable, so peaceable . . . that I swear to your Majesties there is not in the world a better nation." Nevertheless, he said, they should be "made to work, sow and do all that is necessary and to adopt our ways."

Always, assuming our goal was not extermination by deadly force, our object has been to transform the Indians, to make them like ourselves. But if they become like ourselves, if they assimilate, they will no longer be Indians, and there will be no Indian languages, no Indian view of the world, no Indian political communities.

Nor Indian land. Native people feel an attachment to their land, a sense of belonging to a part of the earth, that we can scarcely comprehend. For Native people, their land is not a commodity but the heritage of the community, the dwelling place of generations. It is where they were born, where they will spend their lives, and where they will die. For them to lose their land is a misfortune beyond measure.

By what right did we take their land and subjugate them? Having done so, by what right do we now claim that they should assimilate? Is the argument that, since we took their country—in fact, two whole continents—and reduced them to a condition of lamentable poverty, nothing remains except for them to merge their identity with ours? What excuses did we have? What reasons did we offer to justify taking possession of the New World? Does justice have any claims on us today?

I have thought about these questions. As a lawyer I have been engaged in many cases brought on behalf of Native peoples in Canada. After I became a judge, I conducted the Mackenzie Valley Pipeline Inquiry from 1974 to 1977, travelling throughout Canada's western Arctic to hear the views of Native people and non-Natives about whether a pipeline and energy corridor should be built from the Arctic to the mid-continent, across lands claimed by Native people. In 1979–80 I served as commissioner for Indian and Inuit Health Consultation. I intervened in Canada's constitutional debate in 1981 to urge the restoration of guarantees of aboriginal and treaty rights to the proposed new Canadian Constitution; my intervention led to my departure from the bench. From 1983 to 1985 I conducted the Alaska Native Review Commission, to examine the effect of the land claims settlement for Alaska Natives enacted by the United States Congress in 1971. Since then I have again represented Native causes in the courts.

So, I have heard the arguments many times—indeed, I have made some of them many times. What about the Indians? What is the matter with them? Why do we owe them a living? And so on, and on, the phrases changing little over the decades—indeed, over the centuries. The same attitudes persist.

Nowadays, Native people can and do speak for themselves. This book is an attempt to explain to those of us in the dominant society our ideas about ourselves and about our attitudes towards Native peoples. Those ideas are European because they are derived from Europe, and are held by all of us of European descent and all others who have assimilated to the dominant culture of the New World.

I call this hemisphere "the New World" because five hundred years ago, for Europeans, North and South America were a new world. The encounter between Europe and America raised moral, legal and philosophical questions that are still before us today. True, we and our institutions have prevailed throughout the New World. But the Native people are still here, and they have never surrendered their history or their identity.

It is important for us to know something about that history. In 1992 we commemorate the five hundredth anniversary of Columbus's landfall and the triumph of the European enterprise in the New World. The history that we will celebrate is the history of the progress we have made. That progress has been made at the expense of the Indians; for them that history is one of suffering, of massacre, disease and devastation. Europe has cast a long and terrible shadow over the Native people of the New World. Today they are emerging from beneath that shadow, and they have a tale to tell not only of subjugation but also of survival, for they still live among us, and they have a claim on our consciences, a claim that we should honour the principles by which we profess to live.

If we are to understand who we are, we must know about the history of our encounter with the Native people of the Americas. We cannot judge what it is right to do now without knowing what has gone before.

I do not seek to denigrate the European achievement. Our progress in science and technology is tangible, but our achievement can be observed as well in the emergence of ideas, ideas about the rule of law, about human rights, about the primacy of moral and ethical obligations. The application of these ideas should lead us to a fair accommodation of the claims of the original inhabitants of the New World. What lies in the way of such an accommodation is the persistence of attitudes that have too often triumphed in the past: that superiority in arms entitles one nation to subdue another; that land can be taken from a people if we deem them or their use of land to be deficient; that all cultures should be judged by our own; that injustice, if it is of sufficiently long standing, need not be redressed.

Our history shows that we have always been aware of this unfinished business, that we can still be moved by the voices of the past, which still speak to us of what must be done if Europe's enterprise in the New World is to be true to Europe's own ideals.

In many parts of the New World the Indians have been destroyed, in others they have been removed from their ancestral lands, in still others they have been reduced to poverty. Nevertheless, living on what remains of their tribal territories, Indian people remain connected to ancient values and cultural ways that mark them off from the dominant society. In the dominant society one view of progress and development prevails, in Native communities another. Arising out of their aboriginal occupation of the land, and the persistence of their own beliefs and their way of life, they have in many cases managed to retain their ancestral enclaves and, however attenuated, their institutions of self-government.

We have often predicted their demise, yet they insist upon their continued existence. Indian people have struggled all along to keep their land and their distinctive ideas of land tenure, and have fought to preserve their culture. For Canadians, in 1990, the confrontation between Canadian troops and Mohawk warriors at Oka and Manitoba Native legislator Elijah Harper's determined stance against passage of any constitutional accord that did not acknowledge aboriginal rights were reminders of this Native tenacity. In that same summer of discontent, Indians throughout Ecuador demonstrated in support of their land claims, set up barricades throughout the country and, for the first time in living memory, marched in protest through the streets of Quito, the capital. Indeed, today you cannot pick up a newspaper without reading of Native peoples, in North and South America, seeking to reclaim their birthright.

The Indians have waged—and are waging today—a battle to survive as distinct peoples in our midst. In one way or another, in virtually every country of the New World, indigenous peoples are reminding us that for them 1492 was not the end of history.

CHAPTER I

Las Casas and the Rights of the Indians

During 1975 and 1976 I conducted hearings in northern Canada to examine a proposal to build a gas pipeline and energy corridor along the Mackenzie Valley from the Arctic Ocean to the midcontinent. The Inquiry took me to every village, town and settlement in Canada's western Arctic. More than a thousand persons, Native and non-Native, testified. Government and industry wanted to build the pipeline. Native people of the region—Indians, Métis and Inuit—opposed the pipeline. They wanted a settlement of their land claims first, to preserve their hunting, fishing and trapping economy. They also wanted to secure their right to a measure of self-government. Opposition to the pipeline was seen as opposition to development. The great pipeline project would be an opportunity for Native people to give up a backward way of life and join the modern world.

For two and a half years, I listened to the arguments: This project is the means for you to enter the economic mainstream, your ticket to the wage economy. No, we are not ready; we don't want a project in our valley so big that it will overwhelm us; our land claims must be settled first. To you the pipeline is progress, to us it is a threat to our existence.

Many regarded Native opposition as obstinate, as downright stupid. Others felt it was owing to the influence of outside agitators. There was a reluctance to take Native people seriously, to accept that they, their culture or their beliefs should stand in our way. They, on the other hand, were steadfast in their opposition. To bemused government officials and industrialists, they spoke of the region as their homeland, and of their wish to govern themselves on their own land.

After the Inquiry, on a visit to a secondhand book store, I saw a title, *Aristotle and the American Indians,* by Lewis Hanke. I picked up the book and in it found an account of a debate that took place at Valladolid in Spain in 1550. The arguments put forward echoed those I had just heard, a moral and intellectual controversy that had engaged the Spanish after Columbus claimed the New World. By what right did the Europeans acquire the West Indies, Mexico and Peru? By what right did they subjugate the Indian peoples who lived there? By what right did they require them to repudiate their way of life?

In 1492, the year that Columbus sailed with a commission from King Ferdinand and Queen Isabella, Spanish arms had completed the expulsion of the Moors from the Iberian Peninsula. Following Columbus's voyage, Spaniards soon subjugated the West Indies. By 1521, Cortés had conquered Mexico; by 1532 Pisarro had conquered Peru. Spain, now the possessor of a fabulous overseas empire, was the most powerful nation in Europe.

It had taken the Spaniards seven centuries to expel their Moorish overlords. War with another race, on behalf of Christ, had become a way of life for Spanish men-at-arms. Once the reconquest of Spain was complete, the Spanish soldiery were suddenly without adversaries, yet unsuited to commerce or labour. Providentially, it seemed, the discovery of the New World offered a new adventure; they would not have to put up their swords. Instead, they could pursue their warlike ways against a new enemy.

The Indians of the New World were not, however, Moors; they had not made war on Christians; they were not an occupying power. They lived in a land across the ocean, speaking languages of their own, with their own cultures, their own civilizations. The Spanish had been justified in evicting the Moors from the Spanish homeland. But what right did the Spanish have to conquer the Indians, and to occupy *their* homeland?

The Spaniards came first to the West Indies; they waged a series of campaigns of extermination against the Indians of Hispaniola. On horseback, accompanied by infantry and bloodhounds, the *conquistadores* destroyed almost at will the hunting and gathering tribes of the island. They raped and murdered, sparing neither women nor children. Resistance by the Indians was put down mercilessly. By 1496 the Spaniards were in complete control of the island of Hispaniola. Similar assaults were made on Cuba and other islands of the Caribbean.

The conquistadores came to the New World in the name of the King but also in the name of Jesus. The Church was often their willing instrument in the pillaging of the new lands. Priests accompanying the soldiers, coming upon Indian villages, would read the *Requerimiento* to the Indians, a formal demand, in Spanish, that they adopt the Christian faith. The Requerimiento recited the king's title to the New World, a title granted by the Church. It declared that Jesus was lord of the universe, that he had appointed Saint Peter as Bishop of Rome, and that the pope had bestowed America on the King of Spain.

According to the Requerimiento the Indians were obliged to enter the faith and to acknowledge the king's sovereignty. The Indians did not speak Spanish, so they understood not a word. In any event, they had never heard of Jesus nor the king nor the pope. No time was given for consideration: there had to be immediate compliance. If the Indians refused to acknowledge the authority of the king and the pope, the soldiers would kill them, and as the Requerimiento advised the Indians, "And we protest that the deaths and losses which shall result from this are your fault. . . . " The Indians who were not killed were compelled to leave their homes to become labourers in the mines, field hands and beasts of burden.

The resulting system of forced labour became swiftly entrenched.

o

Introduced in 1502, it was known as the *encomienda*. In the name of the Crown, land was granted to a Spaniard, usually a soldier, and along with it he was allotted Indians to work the land. They were given no choice but to work for him, an obligation known as *ripartimiento*. In return the landowner was required to provide religious training for the Indians. The royal instructions put it baldly: the Indians "are to be compelled to work so that the Kingdom and the Spaniards may be enriched, and the Indians Christianized." In theory, the Indians were to be free and to receive payment for their labour; in fact, they were not free, and received no wages. Although they were not slaves, for they were not bought and sold, their life was one of involuntary servitude.

To the fate of the Indians the Spaniards were indifferent. Historian Gonzalo Fernández de Oviedo y Valdés, himself a conquistador, described them as "naturally lazy and vicious, melancholic, cowardly, and in general a lying, shifty people." He asked, "Who can deny that the use of gun powder against pagans is the burning of incense to Our Lord?" Indeed, the measures taken by Madrid to protect the Indians reveal much about the conquistadores' treatment of them. The Laws of Burgos, enacted by Spain in 1512, provided that "No person. . . . shall dare beat any Indian with sticks, or whip him, or call him a dog, or address him by any name other than his proper name alone." Subjugation of the Indians was accompanied by hideous acts of cruelty. Even today, five centuries on, we shrink from recounting them at any greater length than is necessary to illustrate how appalling they could be.

Here are two accounts, provided by Dominican priests, of Spanish savagery in the Caribbean. The first illustrates how children were treated:

> Some Christians encountered an Indian woman, who was carrying in her arms a child at suck; and since the dog they had with them was hungry, they tore the child from the mother's arms and flung it still living to the dog, who proceeded to devour it before the mother's eyes. . . . When there were among the prisoners some women who had recently given birth, if the new-born babes happened to cry, they seized them by the legs and hurled them against the rocks, or flung them into the jungle so that they would be certain to die there.

The second illustrates relations between Spaniards and the workers in the mines:

> Each of them [the foremen] had made it a practice to sleep with the Indian women who were in his work-force, if they pleased him, whether they were married women or maidens. While the foreman remained in the hut or the cabin with the Indian woman, he sent the husband to dig gold out of the mines; and in the evening, when the wretch returned not only was he beaten or whipped because he had not brought up enough gold, but further, most often, he was bound hand and foot and flung under the bed like a dog, before the foreman lay down, directly over him, with his wife.

The Indians lived and died under inhuman conditions. By 1540 the Indians of the Caribbean had been virtually exterminated. On 8 May 1990, at Veracruz, Mexico, Pope John Paul II said, "The discovery, the conquest and the evangelization [of the New World] occupy a luminous place taken all together, even though they are not without shadows." This is a verdict that can only be reached by slighting history. It is a verdict rejected five centuries ago by the greatest defender of the rights of the Indians the Catholic Church has ever had.

In the days of the Spanish Conquest, just as today, the Catholic Church in Latin America was called upon to speak for the oppressed against the temporal order. The cleric who protested most of all was Bartolomé de Las Casas, father of human rights in the New World, God's angry man of the sixteenth century. *protests for the Indians*

We know only a little about Las Casas. Some fragmentary accounts of his career have come down to us, including encomiums by his admirers and denunciations by his enemies. But his own writings are available to us, and through them his struggle on behalf of the Indians—a struggle that consumed his long life—can be known. He wrote volumes in that cause, and we may judge today by accounts written in his own time of his influence on the way that men thought, if not on the way they acted. No one could be disinterested where Las Casas was concerned. He would not permit it. He was not subtle and insinuating. With Las Casas, there was no middle ground; he was unequivocal, insistent, alarming.

Las Casas had witnessed the preparations in Seville for the second expedition of Columbus. His father and three uncles sailed with Columbus on that voyage. In 1502, Las Casas himself, seeking his own fortune, arrived in Hispaniola, where he acquired an encomienda. In 1510 he became a priest, but he kept his lands and his Indians. In fact, in 1512 he acquired additional lands and Indians when he took part in the conquest of Cuba.

It was not until 1514 that Las Casas repudiated his way of life. He decided that the Spaniards' treatment of the Indians was "unjust and tyrannical." He gave up his encomienda and his Indians and, in a sermon at Sancti Espiritus, the cathedral in Santo Domingo, the capital of the Spanish colonies in the West Indies, condemned his countrymen and the means by which they had gained their fortunes.

In 1515, Las Casas made the first of fourteen journeys to Madrid, where he was granted an audience with King Ferdinand. The king, at Las Casas's urging, established a commission to investigate "the Indian question." How many such commissions have there been since then, undertaken by the European powers in the New World, and by their successor regimes, all of them, like the first, undertaken with a sense of guilt, a measure of goodwill, and in the end a conviction that nothing could be done that might impede the proliferation of European settlement throughout the New World? When the king died, and before it had completed its work, the commission was terminated.

Charles V succeeded Ferdinand. It was to this king that Las Casas was to bring his petitions for the next thirty years. We know a good deal more about Charles V than we do about Las Casas. Charles's father was Philip of Burgundy, his mother Joanna, third child of Ferdinand and Isabella. Charles was raised in the Netherlands, where he had, as a child of six, succeeded to that throne. In 1518, two years after the death of King Ferdinand, Spain recognized Charles as its king. In the same year, he succeeded to the throne of the Hapsburg kingdoms. In 1520, he was crowned Holy Roman Emperor.

In that same year Las Casas had his first audience with the new king. Las Casas revealed to the king the atrocities being committed against the Indians by Spain. He was uncompromising in his denunciation.

> Your Majesty will find out that there are no Christians in these lands; instead, there are demons. There are neither ser-

vants of God nor of the King. Because, in truth the great obstacle to my being able to bring the Indians from war-making to a peaceful way of life, and to bring the knowledge of God to those Indians who are peaceful is the harsh and cruel treatment of these Indians by the Spanish Christians. For which scabrous and better reason no word can be more hateful to those Indians than the word Christians which. . . . in their language. . . . means Demons. And without a doubt they are right, because the actions of these Governors are neither Christian nor humane but are actions of the devil.

The king's empire in Europe was already becoming dependent on the income from the West Indies. Cortés had already landed in Mexico; soon the Aztec empire would be Spain's. Within little more than a decade Peru and its gold would fall into the hands of Spain. Charles could not, without the loss of the riches that would make his kingdom the wealthiest in Europe, accede to Las Casas's demands.

It is remarkable, nevertheless, how far this thoughtful monarch was prepared to go. Charles was aware of the magnitude of Spain's discoveries in the New World and of the issues that they raised. On this occasion he told his advisers they must work out a plan for the governance of the colonies in the New World "without force of arms." Pious? Fraudulent? Perhaps. There is, however, reason to believe that the king was on the side of Las Casas, that he genuinely wished to see a humane regime established in his overseas possessions. But even he could not resist the advance by Europe into the New World, and Spain was Europe's spearhead.

Las Casas told the king that the Indians were "by nature. . . . most humble, patient, and peaceable, holding no grudges, free from embroilments, neither excitable nor quarrelsome." They were not like that, of course, and it is by no means certain that Las Casas believed they were. What is not open to doubt is that Las Casas himself was not 'humble, patient, and peaceable.' He was argumentative, rancorous, often impossible. But how could his defence of the Indians have been sustained for so long—through the reigns of three kings and for fifty years—except by a sense of outrage that could not be extinguished, even though it might from time to time threaten to consume his judgement?

Las Casas has not been a hero to Spain. Spain holds him respon-

sible for the Black Legend, a name given to the tale of Spanish cruelty
in the New World. In fact, the Black Legend was the work of many
writers, Las Casas being only one, though undoubtedly the most important. But Las Casas's Spanish critics forget that Las Casas was
himself a Spaniard. They forget, too, that it was the king of Spain,
Charles V, whose regime allowed Las Casas to proclaim his opposition to the conquest, urging the king to check the advance of his empire. Furthermore, Las Casas's remonstrances were in some measure
heeded. Compare this monarchy with the regimes of Latin America
today. Are any of them entitled to claim that in their treatment of
the Indians they are the true heirs of Charles V and Las Casas?

By the early sixteenth century, Spain had subjugated the Indians
of the West Indies. When the Spaniards invaded the mainland, they
encountered the great empires of the Aztecs and the Incas. When
Cortés landed at Veracruz on the eastern shores of Mexico, a new
era began.

Reaching the Aztec capital of Tenochtitlán, the Spaniards were
astonished to find a beautiful city, larger than Madrid, the centre of
an empire of eleven million people. In Peru, where the Incas ruled,
the Spaniards discovered a realm of six million Indians, boasting
roads and irrigation systems, all built high in the Andes. Yet the
Spaniards were determined to destroy what the Aztecs and the Incas
had built. The Spanish regime of cruelty and death, begun in the
Caribbean, was carried into Mexico and Peru.

As a boy, I read Prescott's account of the conquests of Mexico and
Peru, the grandest adventures of the Spanish conquistadores. Today
I wonder, how have these helmeted adventurers and these plumed
Indian nobles affected the history of our relations with the Indians?
How important is it that their images are fixed in our imagination?

The Spanish conquests were fabulous, unprecedented in
history—so swift and sudden as to seem foreordained. Cortés, with
four hundred men and fifteen horses, established dominion over the
empire of the Aztecs; Pisarro, with even fewer men, dispatched the
Inca king and acquired his kingdom. Although the Indians of Mexico
and Peru survived, they did so in servitude and sorrow.

When Cortés landed at Veracruz in 1519, he was well received by
the local Indians, who had only recently been brought under the rule
of the Aztecs. Cortés sent a message to Moctezuma, the Aztec em-

peror, asking permission to visit his capital. In response, Moctezuma sent a delegation to welcome Cortés, consisting of Aztec nobles accompanied by porters bearing gifts made of gold. Bernal Díaz del Castillo, one of Cortés's men, wrote:

> The first article presented was a wheel like a sun, as big as a cartwheel, with many sorts of pictures on it, the whole of fine gold and a wonderful thing to behold. . . . Then were brought twenty golden ducks, beautifully worked and very natural looking, and many articles of gold in the shape of tigers and lions and monkeys. . . . all in beautiful hollow work of fine gold.

This was what the Spaniards had been seeking: gold, and here it was in abundance.

Cortés soon realized that he had encountered a powerful empire, but he resolved to go forward. He burned his ships to ensure that his soldiers had no choice but to accompany him and proceeded inland, intending to march to the Valley of Mexico. Along the way Cortés and his men had to battle the Indians of Tlaxcala. The Tlaxcalas had never before faced steel swords, crossbows, firearms and light artillery, and had never before seen horses or men on horseback. Moreover, the Spanish were disciplined soldiers, accustomed to making war. Cortés defeated the far more numerous Tlaxcala, then made an alliance with them against the Aztecs. In fact, Cortés found that many of the subject tribes were ready to rise against their Aztec masters.

Moctezuma, alarmed at Cortés's progress, invited the Spaniard to visit him at Tenochtitlán. Cortés arrived at the capital at the head of his Spanish infantry, accompanied by a force of five thousand Tlaxcala. There, for the first time, Europeans saw Tenochtitlán, the city built on a lake. Bernal Díaz del Castillo takes up the story:

> We were amazed on account of the great towers and buildings rising from the water, and all built of masonry. And some of our soldiers even asked whether the things that we saw were not a dream. Gazing on such wonderful sights, we did not know what to say, or whether what appeared before us was real, for on one side, on the land, there were great cities, and in

the lake ever so many more, and the lake itself was crowded with canoes. . . . and in front of us stood the great City of Mexico, and we—we did not even number four hundred soldiers.

Cortés entered the city unaccompanied by his Indian allies. For a time relations were cordial; Cortés even sought to convert Moctezuma to Christianity.

Then Cortés struck. On a visit to Moctezuma's palace, accompanied by thirty armed men, he took the emperor prisoner and carried him off to the Spaniards' quarters. The Aztecs were at first paralysed by this bold act, but soon retaliated. The Aztec nobles tried to expel the Spaniards. During the struggle Moctezuma, still in Spanish custody, was killed. Cortés and his men retreated from the city, under attack from every side, sustaining great losses, until they managed to reach safety at Tlaxcala.

There Cortés incited revolt throughout the Aztec empire, organized a new army, built a fleet of brigantines to enable him to attack the Aztec capital from the water, and, together with his Indian allies, marched again on Tenochtitlán. He forced an entry to the city and attacked with his fleet along the canals, his cannon firing across the causeways. The Aztecs defended the capital bravely, under the leadership of Cuauhtémoc, the last emperor of the Aztecs. But the outcome was no longer in doubt. Once Cuauhtémoc was captured, Aztec resistance was ended. With the fall of Tenochtitlán, the Spaniards plundered the capital. Cortés was now master of the Aztec empire.

Cortés's conquest of the Aztec empire is celebrated as a triumph of European arms, courage and technology. Surely it demonstrates the superiority of Europe over the peoples of the New World. How else could a comparative handful of men overthrow an empire? Of course, there were many reasons for the triumph of Cortés. The initial shock resulting from the arrival of strange and powerful men from across the ocean, and the paralysis it induced at the centre of the empire, the advantage that armed soldiers on horseback possessed over the Aztec warriors on foot, and the fact that the Spanish infantry were armed with muskets—all these made the victory possible.

Then, too, there was the disaffection among Moctezuma's subject peoples. His was, after all, a theocratic empire only recently established. The tribes were ready to revolt. But what explanation is there for the fecklessness displayed by Moctezuma in the face of the Spanish incursion? Some think that the Aztecs may have been prisoners of a mystic world. Perhaps Moctezuma thought Cortés was Quetzalcoatl, the bearded god of the Toltecs, now returned after five centuries. Perhaps Moctezuma had an intimation that Cortés represented a greater power than his own, with weaponry the Aztecs could not match, that he represented a race who, having discovered Moctezuma's empire, would never rest until they defeated him. In any event, Spain's conquest of the Aztecs did much to entrench in the minds of Europeans the certainty of their destiny in America.

Pisarro's name is linked with that of Cortés. Like Cortés, with only a few hundred soldiers, he captured an empire. In Panama news had come, as early as 1523, of an Indian empire in the Andes, a realm of gold beyond calculation. Francisco Pisarro was the first to organize an expedition to sail south along the Pacific coast in search of this land of the Incas. On his third voyage, in 1531, Pisarro sailed with 180 men and twenty-seven horses. When he reached Peru civil war had broken out among the Incas; landing at Tumbes, he found the city had already been destroyed.   — *Only 100 yrs old*

The empire of the Incas, established along the highlands stretching from Ecuador to Bolivia, was no more than a hundred years old. It was an astounding achievement: the roads through the mountains, the storehouses, the agricultural terraces, the cities built in the clouds. Like the Aztecs, the Incas had subjugated a host of other Indian peoples.

Pisarro landed at a propitious moment. In 1527, the Inca king, Huayna Capac, had died. At his death, he had divided the empire between his sons, Atahualpa and Huáscar. These two fought. Atahualpa took Huáscar prisoner and captured Cuzco, the Inca capital. On learning that Atahualpa was visiting Cajamarca in the mountains of northern Peru, Pisarro and his men left the coast and marched into the mountains, along the roads built by the Incas, to seek out the Inca king.

Atahualpa knew of Pisarro's march, but he made no attempt to molest Pisarro and his men as they made the ascent into the Andes. When Pisarro arrived at Cajamarca, he found the city empty, the king encamped at the hot springs nearby. Pisarro occupied and fortified the central plaza, then sent an emissary to Atahualpa, inviting him to visit the deserted city. Atahualpa agreed, and announced that he and his followers would not be armed. Pisarro, like Cortés, decided that he must make the emperor his captive.

When Atahualpa, with thousands of retainers, entered the empty plaza of Cajamarca, Pisarro's chaplain, Father Valverde, approached the king and, through an interpreter, sought to convert him to Christianity. When the king treated this as impudence, the priest ran to Pisarro, urging him to attack, and absolving him and his troops from any blame for the bloodshed that would ensue.

At Pisarro's signal the Spanish cavalry supported by the infantry emerged from hiding and charged the unarmed Indians, killing thousands, including many of the nobles. Some of Atahualpa's followers sought to protect him, but they were swiftly cut down by the Spanish swordsmen. The remainder of the king's followers fled. Now Pisarro had Atahualpa in his custody, and through him, control of the empire. It was all over in half an hour.

Atahualpa soon realized that his captors sought gold above all things. He offered to provide the Spaniards with a roomful of gold if they would release him; Pisarro agreed. At Atahualpa's direction, the Incas brought gold to Cajamarca from all over the kingdom, a treasure equivalent to half a century of European production. Once the roomful of gold had been supplied, the Spaniards reneged on their promise to give Atahualpa his freedom. No doubt the Spaniards realized that the king, if he were restored to his people, would have them at his mercy. So, the Spaniards held a trial, found Atahualpa guilty of crimes invented for the occasion and condemned him to be burned alive. The egregious Father Valverde told Atahualpa that he would be strangled, not burned alive, if he agreed to be baptized. The king agreed, was baptized, then put to death by a cord passed around his neck. The capture and execution of Atahualpa, like that of Moctezuma, transferred supreme authority over the empire into Spanish hands with a single stroke. After the murder of Atahualpa, Pisarro appointed the king's half-brother, Manco Inca, to succeed him, and marched to Cuzco.

It was Manco Inca, the puppet emperor, however, who was to lead the revolt of the Incas. In 1536, Manco Inca escaped Cuzco on a ruse, and assembled 20,000 warriors. They besieged the Spanish in Cuzco for a year, coming very close to defeating them. But the siege could not be maintained, and Manco Inca took refuge in the inaccessible mountains of Vilcabamba. In the territory still under his control, Manco established a neo-Inca state. It was not until 1572 that Vilcabamba fell to the Spaniards. Tupac Amaru, the last Inca king, was captured and brought to Cuzco, where he was beheaded in the central plaza.

The Spanish conquerors extended the encomienda system to Mexico and Peru. This meant forced labour and the exaction of tribute. The Indians, as the only available labour force, were indispensable to the economic advance of the new colonies. The conquistadores were not farmers. Without the Indians the conquered lands had little value. As Columbus had earlier written:

> The Indians of [Hispaniola] are its riches, because they are the ones who dig and make the bread and other victuals of the Christians, and take out the gold of their mines, and do all the other tasks and labour of men and beasts of burden.

The only way that the Spanish regime in Mexico and Peru could thrive was by keeping the Indian under the domination of the Spaniards, by requiring his labour and seizing his land. The encomienda made possible the formation in Latin America of an economically powerful, exclusive social class. Native societies had to be subordinated to Spanish authority. Mass killing and terror were employed by the Spanish to ensure their ascendancy. In Mexico and Peru the Indians were dispatched without remorse. The identity of the victim was irrelevant. Far from the central government in Madrid, all prohibitions gave way. But distance does not account for everything. Nor does the suggestion that the conquistadores were the flotsam of Spain. Nor was it simply craving for gold.

Why then did Spaniards feel free to murder and rob, to commit acts of unspeakable cruelty? Why did the condition of the Indians not arouse their compassion? The answer, I think, lies in the suddenness of their victories. The Spaniards saw the ease of their conquest as proof of the superiority of European civilization and of the Christian religion. The Indians had been defeated because they were static, backward societies that could not react effectively when challenged. They succumbed swiftly and just as swiftly they gave up their own gods and adopted Christianity. To the European conquerors, the Indians had no story to tell; indeed, insofar as they were without a written language, they had to depend on Europeans to give an account of their history and their beliefs. The persistence of Latin American disregard for Indian rights stems from these early encounters.

I have given this brief account of the Spanish conquests because I think they remain in the conscious or subconscious minds of all of us. The images they portray go a long way towards explaining Spain's unwillingness—and ours—to accord Indians a meaningful place in the political firmament. For the Indians the conquest was a cosmic tragedy; for the Spaniards the conquest was not only the means by which they had taken possession of the Indian lands, it was also by its swiftness and completeness justification itself for their overlordship. Yet, for some among the conquerors such justification did not come easily. Moral compunction demanded that Spain's right to sovereignty over the New World and its peoples be formally defined, that the regime of the conquistadores be challenged. Bartolomé de Las Casas was to make this his life's work.

CHAPTER 2

The Debate at Valladolid

Here is how Las Casas described the Spaniards' assault on the peoples of the New World, in his *Brief Account* written in 1542:

> . . . into this sheepfold, into this land of meek outcasts, there came some Spaniards who immediately behaved like ravening beasts, wolves, tigers, or lions that had been starved for many days. And Spaniards have behaved in no other way during the past 40 years down to the present time, for they are still acting like ravening beasts, killing, terrorizing, afflicting, torturing and destroying the native peoples, doing all this with the strangest and most varied new methods of cruelty, never seen or heard of before. . . .

According to Las Casas, millions of Indians had been slain. Why did these Christians destroy "such an infinite number of souls?" Their aim, he said was "to acquire gold . . . to swell themselves with riches . . . and to rise to a high estate disproportionate to their merits." The cause? According to Las Casas, " . . . their insatiable greed and ambition, the greatest ever seen in the world, is the cause of their villainies." If his cause had not been humane, his work profound and his life prophetic, Las Casas's denunciation of the acts of his countrymen would have seemed unbearably shrill:

> . . . our Spaniards have no more consideration for them than beasts. . . . But I should not say "than beasts" for, thanks be to God, they have treated beasts with some respect; I should say instead like excrement on the public squares.

Such criticism was intolerable to Spanish soldiers and settlers. But a more insidious and a more profound source of disquiet lay in the implications of Las Casas's attack on the legitimacy of Spanish rule.

Las Casas held that Spain had the right to enter the lands of the Indians only to Christianize them. Spain's title to its kingdom in the New World depended on the faithfulness with which it carried out its missionary task. But there had been no attempt to convert the Indians by peaceful means; instead, a military conquest by terror had been undertaken. As for the Requerimiento, Las Casas said he did not know whether to laugh or weep. "Suppose," he said, "the Moors or the Turks had come with the same injunction declaring Mohammed the ruler of the World, were they [the Spaniards] to believe it?" To Las Casas, the Spaniards had no right to the rewards of their daring.

Las Casas was not alone in questioning the legitimacy of Spanish claims in the Americas. In Spain—and throughout Europe—many scholars considered the fundamental issues of political theory raised by the discovery of the New World. How could it be that Europeans are entitled to the lands of people far away who have held them for thousands of years? The consideration of these questions did not take place in a vacuum; there was a natural tendency to justify the accomplished fact. Spain had taken the New World by force, and was not about to relinquish it. The prevailing disposition was to declare that this was as it should be. Yet the competing theory, advanced by Las Casas, which placed Spain's claim in jeopardy, was heard and considered and, in fact, from time to time prevailed.

In 1494 the pope had divided the New World between Spain and Portugal. The king of Spain, like Las Casas, regarded this donation of the Holy See as the origin of his title, as an unlimited grant of sovereignty. Las Casas, however, argued that the pope had no jurisdiction over non-Christians. The pope and those who ruled by his authority could not force pagans to accept Christianity; they might only teach them the falsity of their gods and the truth of Christ. Las Casas believed that all men must be free, that God intended this as an essential attribute of man; he declared, "Mankind is one."

The pope, argued Las Casas, had no authority to take from pagans their lands or their freedom; he might only give to Christian kings authority to preach the faith to such infidels. Only for such purposes might the king claim the Indians as his subjects. If he failed, or if his soldiers failed to spread the faith by Christ-like methods, his title to these new lands was invalidated. As Spain had manifestly failed in this, it followed that, to secure his title, the king must undo the wrongs committed by the conquistadores in his name, and restore to the Indians their lands, the wealth taken from them, and their own rulers. Not to put too fine a point on it, Las Casas was in his own time an advocate of Indian land claims and Indian sovereignty.

These were radical propositions. Why was Las Casas allowed to urge them? Although the Church punished heresy—the Inquisition was active in Spain at the time—the Church did not punish those, like Las Casas, who urged the implementation of Christ's teaching in secular affairs.

In 1537, Las Casas and his fellow Dominicans decided to demonstrate that the Indians could be Christianized without the use of force. Bringing farm implements along with their bibles, they undertook, through peaceful means, to convert the Indians of a part of Guatemala; they called the colony the Land of True Peace, or Verapaz. At first they were successful; the Indians agreed to become subjects of the Spanish king, and self-governing Indian farming communities were established. If the conquistadores were to enter the colony, all would be lost. Yet this is what happened. A decree excluding the Spanish soldiery from the land was revoked, and soon the encomienda was entrenched in Verapaz.

Las Casas believed that his experiment had proven that the Indians could be won over to Christ and to the king by reason and by example. Convinced that what had been achieved in the Land of True Peace could be achieved throughout the Spanish colonies in the New World, he urged the king to abolish the encomienda. King Charles, to the astonishment of his court and the consternation of his subjects overseas, decreed that no further encomiendas would be granted, and that when those already holding encomiendas died, their Indians would be released from any further obligations to their masters.

These were the New Laws announced in Seville in 1542. Henceforth, no Spaniards were to take Indians into their service by way of the encomienda. The hand of Las Casas can be seen in the concluding sentence of the document: "The inhabitants of the Indian lands are to be treated in every respect as free subjects of the Crown of Castille: for there exists no difference between the latter and the former."

When Charles V promulgated the New Laws, he may have thought that, at a stroke, he would put an end to the encomienda system. In fact, the king was virtually powerless to enforce his will on the now numerous Spanish colonists. Spaniards in Peru rebelled against the king, subsiding only after Spain made it plain that the clause abolishing the encomienda would not be enforced. In Mexico the colonists came to the verge of rebellion. Spanish officials in the New World sided with the colonists. They could not enforce the New Laws against the will of the Spanish settlers.

Nevertheless, the mere fact of the enactment of the New Laws is breathtaking. Imagine an empire in which a cleric, by the sheer force of his personality and the weight of his argument, persuades a king to revoke the rights claimed by his own subjects, now grown powerful, in the lands that produced the wealth flowing into Spain in each of the galleons entering the harbour at Seville.

What were Charles's motives for enacting the New Laws? No doubt they were mixed. Charles was, after all, a man who well knew the world of practical politics. When Pope Paul III, in 1537, declared that the Indians were entitled to retain not only their liberty but also their property, Charles had him annul the declaration within a year.

The New Laws were designed to protect the Indians. But they served also as a means of enlarging royal authority, to check the power of the conquistadores. When the settlers refused to submit to the New Laws, however, Charles had to give way. He could not risk rebellion in these profitable possessions. His successors faced the same predicament. Spanish America was to remain, notwithstanding the decrees emanating from Madrid, a regime of gold and greed, silver and serfdom.

Despite the failure of the Crown to protect the Indians, the Indians continued to look to Madrid as their champion. When Tupac Amaru II led a rebellion in the eighteenth century in Peru, taking the name of the last Inca emperor, he claimed to do so on behalf of the Spanish Crown. In Canada and the United States, the Native people still insist on their special relationship with the federal government, which in both countries inherited the obligations the British Crown had assumed towards the Native people.

Charles was not simply a bemused monarch who allowed controversy to fester at court in order to keep his ecclesiastical advisers at one remove. He found the slaughter in the Indies truly horrifying: whole peoples were being destroyed. The king's subjects, acting in his name, were engaged in the deliberate and systematic destruction of millions of Indians.

Las Casas, finding that the Crown could not check the cruelty of the conquistadores, decided to use the sanctions of the Church itself. After the revocation of the New Laws, Las Casas was made Bishop of Chiapas, a poor province in southern Mexico. Arriving there, he instructed his priests to refuse the sacraments to any soldier, plantation owner or mine owner, who would not sign a notarized promise to free his Indians.

In Chiapas, threats of excommunication did not, any more than the prospect of prosecution for disobedience to the Crown, deter the settlers from continuing to force the Indians to work for them, for on this arrangement depended the economy erected by the Spaniards. The intractability of the economic arrangements, even though not even a half-century old, was the crucial factor. The Spaniards were simply not willing to surrender what they had taken. The encomienda defined the relationship between the Spaniard and the Indian. It made one of them a lord, the other a serf; it made one of them wealthy, the other poor. The Spaniard would resist any attempt to alter this state of affairs. This was the imprinting of Latin America: the raising up of the Europeans, the degradation of the Indians.

Tiring of what they considered to be his meddlesome sanctimony, the landowners of Chiapas denounced Las Casas for high treason. In 1547 he was required to return to Madrid, never to see the New

World again. But Las Casas's career was not ended. Until his death in 1566, he served as the advocate of the Indians before the king and the Council of the Indies. He also wrote his most enduring works during these years. Nor could it have been apparent to him when he left Mexico that the greatest drama of his career lay ahead of him, for he was to confront Juan Ginés de Sepúlveda, Spain's most famous philosopher, in a debate the echoes of which can still be heard throughout the New World.

In 1550 Charles V summoned a junta of the most learned men in Spain—clerics, lawyers and other scholars—to the city of Valladolid. He urged them to consider Las Casas's challenge to the Conquest. The point on which the king sought advice was: "How can conquests, discoveries and settlements [in my name] be made to accord with justice and reason?" While the junta deliberated, Charles ordered a moratorium on further expeditions to the New World.

Sepúlveda and Las Casas addressed the junta in turn, though they did not meet face to face. Las Casas's speech lasted five days. The debate was far-reaching, encompassing the nature of man, the law of nations and the legitimacy of the Conquest.

Sepúlveda adopted the view of Aristotle that some races are inferior to others, that some men are born to slavery. By this reasoning, the Europeans, a superior race, were justified in subjugating the Indians, an inferior race. To Sepúlveda, the Indians were barbarians. They belonged to the same species as Europeans, but they were retarded in their development. The Indians' inferiority came naturally, and their subjection did no injustice to them.

This theory seemed satisfactory as far as the Indians of the Caribbean were concerned. But how to explain the Aztecs and the Incas, the great cities and vast empires of the cordillera? The Spaniards were city dwellers. The building of cities was one of the indications of civilization. Were not Tenochtitlán and Cuzco the work of true men?

The Aztecs and the Incas, however, did not behave as civilized men, for they engaged in human sacrifice and in the eating of human flesh. For Europeans, human sacrifice and the eating of human flesh cancelled out any attributes of civilization that the Indians may have possessed. Sepúlveda argued, therefore, that these inhuman practices justified war against the Indians of Mexico and Peru.

Las Casas admitted that these practices occurred among the Indians. But they were, he said, the Indians' way of proving their devotion to their gods—an indication of reverence and submission that might be equated to the true holiness of devout Christians, just as it had been with Abraham and Isaac. In any event, he said, human sacrifice did not justify "the destruction of whole kingdoms and cities."

Sepúlveda said that the Indians:

> . . . require, by their own nature and in their own interests, to be placed under the authority of civilized and virtuous princes or nations, so that they may learn, from the might, wisdom, and law of their conquerors, to practise better morals, worthier customs and a more civilized way of life. . . . Compare then those blessings enjoyed by Spaniards of prudence, genius, magnanimity, temperance, humanity, and religion with those of the *homunculi* [little men] in whom you will scarcely find even vestiges of humanity, who not only possess no science but who also lack letters and preserve no monument of their history except certain vague and obscure reminiscences of some things in certain paintings. Neither do they have written laws, but barbaric institutions and customs. They do not even have private property.

He went on:

> The bringing of iron alone compensates for all the gold and silver taken from America. To the immensely valuable iron may be added other Spanish contributions such as wheat, barley, other cereals and vegetables, horses, mules, asses, oxen, sheep, goats, pigs, and an infinite variety of trees. Any one of these greatly exceeds the usefulness the barbarians derived from gold and silver taken by the Spaniards. All these blessings are in addition to writing, books, culture, excellent laws, and that one supreme benefit which is worth more than all others combined: the Christian religion.

In fact, Sepúlveda relied as much on European superiority in technology, on its duty to bring economic development to the Indians, as he did on the blessings of Christianity. He concluded:

> Those who try to prevent Spanish expeditions from bringing all these advantages to the Indians are not favouring them,

as they like to believe, but are really . . . depriving the Indian of many excellent products and instruments without which they will be greatly retarded in their development.

Las Casas, on the other hand, regarded the Indians as people with an evolved culture, with their own social, economic and religious institutions. He urged that the Indians were rational beings, fit to be compared to the Greeks and Romans: "All the peoples of the world are men." His defence of the Indians was not based on mere sentiment but on observation of Indian society. In the debate he described their religion and mores, their social relations, their political system. He sought to counter the stereotype of primitive savages advanced by Sepúlveda.

Las Casas dealt in turn with the Indian economy, architecture and religion. He sought to demonstrate that Indian culture, customs and institutions deserved respect on their own terms. All the peoples of the world might form part of the body of Christ through His Church.

Sepúlveda's hierarchical idea of man was derived from Aristotle, Las Casas's idea of the equality of man from Christ. Las Casas exclaimed: "Aristotle, farewell! From Christ, the eternal truth, we have the commandment 'You must love your neighbor as yourself'."

Here was the very debate that I heard centuries later in the Mackenzie Valley Pipeline Inquiry. The protagonists had changed, the appeal to Christian principles was no longer made, but the appeal to technological progress still formed the centrepiece of the case for the pipeline. Present still was the same inability to comprehend the Native view, and the same appeal by Native people to their own cultural legitimacy, but this time advanced by Native people throughout the valley and not by a foreign champion.

King Charles's junta never did reach a formal decision. What were they to do? How could the clock ever be set back? They could hardly annul the conquest of the Indies. What could the king himself do? He had already been obliged to agree that the New Laws would not be enforced, or face the loss of his empire. He had no choice but to allow expeditions to the New World to be resumed. Soon after, Charles V gave up his throne and entered a monastery, to be succeeded by his son, Philip II. Events overtook the Native people once more.

At the beginning of Las Casas's crusade a bare possibility had existed that the principles he urged might have been adopted as the basis for Spanish rule in the Americas. But as the Spanish conquest proceeded, gaining more and more territory and yielding more and more revenue, the prospects of such a regime dwindled to the vanishing point. With the accession to the throne of Philip II, the influence of Las Casas and his followers diminished. Philip, faced with a financial crisis, sought to augment royal revenue from the Indies; this meant exacting more tribute from the Indians. Indeed, Philip proclaimed that the Indians still alive would have to pay tribute for those who had died.

Las Casas had sought to save the Indians. In this, he no doubt recognized his life's goal. The Vatican has not canonized him, nor is it likely to. He did not abjure the life of the world; rather, he rejoiced in it: the preparation of petitions, the writing of tracts, the clashes with his enemies, the debates at court. He was every bit as caught up in the events of his time as were his adversaries.

Above all, Las Casas was a passionate man. He accused the conquistadores of hideous crimes, challenged the Spaniard's claim to the lands of the Indians, and prophesied the downfall of Spain for looting the wealth of the New World. In his own fashion he was like the conquistadores: unafraid, willing to match himself and his cause against enormous odds, reckless of his own life and—his enemies still say—of the truth.

Yet, despite his advocacy on behalf of the Indians, Las Casas remained a European. He did not think that in the end the Indians should be left alone. He believed that the Indians should be Christianized and that they should submit to Spanish rule. Where he disagreed profoundly with his countrymen was about methods, urging that Spain's rule must be benign.

It is said that Europe brought to America an idea—the idea of individual autonomy—in substitution for the mass subjection of the people to the monolithic empires of the Aztecs and the Incas. But the Indians were not to enjoy individual autonomy under Spain, and their collectivities were broken on the wheel of Spanish cruelty.

The contempt for and indifference towards Indians which countenanced the savagery of the conquistadores has persisted; the conquistadores' legacy is our refusal in our own time to take Indian culture seriously, our disregard for Indian assertions of their rights as peoples, our view that we have an absolute right to appropriate their wealth.

Throughout the New World, since Cortés and Pisarro, men have sought riches at the frontier. Even since those days, men have wished for another Moctezuma's treasure, another Atahualpa to be ransomed. From the beginning the conquerors wished the conquered to understand that the new order must be European, that there would be no place for Indian institutions and beliefs.

The image of the victories of Cortés and Pisarro has lingered in our minds ever since: the inability of the Indians to defend themselves, their incapacity to make war effectively. Today, two peoples live side by side; one rules, the other is impoverished. It has been so for five hundred years. Whites still think of the Indian as what he was—or what they conceive him to have been. No possibility of change is considered except change that makes the Indian a White man. Historians of the United States omit the Indian from their books after the last battles of the Plains. Some of the nation-states of Latin America have claimed that their populations no longer include any Indians, that Native culture and identity have merged in that of the dominant society.

In fact, there have been two peoples, two races, two streams of history, of historical consciousness, that have become mingled. The question that emerged at the outset of European occupation—by what right did one race take the land belonging to another race and subjugate them?—has not vanished; it persists today. Throughout the Americas, Native people insist that their condition and their claims must have a place on the political agenda.

We cannot do justice to the Native peoples unless we are prepared to acknowledge the cruelty, compromise, and indifference that disfigure the history of the New World. Our political and economic ideologies have not been able to account for the Indians. Native people have demonstrated that the world cannot altogether be classified according to ideological dogma, nor explained solely by economic theory. Native people are not simply a rural proletariat, nor just another ethnic minority. Neither can we explain their resistance, their refusal to assimilate.

In his own time Las Casas's voice was not heeded. Once the locus of Spain's enterprise shifted from the West Indies to the mainland, once the wealth of Mexico and Peru had been exposed, the dream of conquest, the opportunity to become masters of the New World, the lure of gold and silver overwhelmed his pleas on behalf of the Indians and overwhelmed the Indians as well. For the Europeans, then as now, superiority in arms, in science and technology, gave them the power to subdue the Indians, and with such power came the means to take possession of them and of their land.

Las Casas insisted that the struggle for justice in the New World was not only waged on behalf of the Indians. It was also a moral issue vital to Spain, to its idea of itself as a Christian nation. Today, this same struggle is vital not only to the Native peoples but also to the nation-states of the New World. For we, like sixteenth-century Spain, have our principles: we profess to believe in the rule of law, in the self-determination of peoples, and in human rights. Las Casas insisted upon speaking his own truth. In this he still speaks to us all and for us all.

CHAPTER 3

Disease and Death

In May 1990 I was invited to be keynote speaker at the Circumpolar Health Conference in Whitehorse, Yukon Territory. I wondered what I, a lay person in health matters, could say to the five hundred health professionals who were to attend. My own experience in northern Canada and in Alaska had made me aware that the gravest health issues in the Arctic and sub-Arctic regions of North America related to the Native peoples. These are not simply questions of disease, its prevention and cure. They are a cluster of social pathologies that threaten the lives of Native persons and undermine the social life of Native communities. But those attending the conference would know all this. So what could I say? I decided to go back to the beginning, to try to trace the malaise to its origins in the coming of the Europeans to the New World.

European contempt and indifference towards Indians and Indian culture have persisted into our own time, though today their outward manifestation takes a different form than it did five hundred years ago. In the same way, the destruction that the Europeans brought is still with us today, though in a different form. For the impact of the advent of the Europeans was not limited to the regime of violence that they brought to the New World. They also brought European diseases, which irrupted among Indian peoples with no history of exposure to them and no immunity against them.

Smallpox arrived in the West Indies in 1518. From there it travelled to the mainland. Starting at Veracruz, it swept through the country. The disease was unknown in Mexico, and the Indians, who had no resistance to it, died by the hundreds of thousands. The epidemic may have been one reason why the Aztecs did not pursue and slaughter the Spaniards on their flight from Tenochtitlán. Certainly, by the time the Spaniards returned to lay siege to the Aztec capital, the city was filled with the dead. The pestilence disrupted the whole empire. It may have been the terrible toll of European disease that, more than any other factor, made Spain's victory possible. The voices of the survivors tell of the cataclysm that overtook them:

> Great was the stench of death. After our fathers and grandfathers succumbed, half the people fled to the fields. The dogs and vultures devoured the bodies. . . . So it was that we became orphans, oh, my sons! . . . We were born to die.

Disease, once established, spread swiftly, often preceding the Spaniards along their path of conquest. Smallpox crept down the spine of Central America and into the Andes. Pisarro's conquest of Peru was not, perhaps, foreordained; it was expedited by the pathogens that had gone before. As early as 1523, a decade before Pisarro's encounter with Atahualpa, smallpox was depopulating the empire of the Incas. By the time Pisarro's ships reached the coast at Tumbes, the Inca king, Huayna Capac, had died from the disease.

Before Columbus, the Europeans themselves suffered greatly from recurring epidemics of disease. But their losses, though significant, had not been catastrophic. Over hundreds of years these waves of disease produced in survivors a resistance to reinfection, a relative immunity that enabled the conquistadores and the settlers who followed them to survive the plagues they brought with them to the Americas.

The Native population of the New World, by comparison, had remained free of the epidemic diseases that ravaged the Old World. The ancestors of the peoples of the New World had crossed the Bering land bridge long before most infectious diseases had taken hold in Europe and Asia. The diseases they carried with them vanished during their migration through the Arctic "cold screen."

Once they arrived in the New World, Indians (and the Eskimos who travelled across the land bridge after them) were unlikely hosts for the development of new diseases. Because many of them were nomads, they were not prey to the "diseases of filth" that flourished in settled communities. They lived in small, isolated bands and were therefore less likely to spread diseases over large geographical areas. They kept few domesticated animals to attract parasites. Even when the great Indian empires arose and large concentrations of populations emerged in Mexico and Peru, there appears to have been little illness; Aztec histories refer to mass death only in connection with famine, and that was rare. As a result the peoples of North and South America were, in comparison to the rest of the world, remarkably healthy.

With the arrival of the conquistadores came diseases that devastated whole Indian populations. A multitude of plagues reached them during the sixteenth and seventeenth centuries, the entire catalogue of European disease: viruses such as smallpox, chickenpox, measles and influenza; bacterial infections such as pneumonia and scarlet fever; and diseases, like yellow fever and typhus, transmitted by outside agents.

Smallpox epidemics swept through Indian villages, leaving death and debilitation in their wake. Six months after Cortés's victorious entry into Tenochtitlán, hardly a village in Mexico had not been devastated by the first wave of disease. In the words of one of the Spanish chroniclers, the Indians "died in heaps, like bedbugs."

New infections followed swiftly: the effect was cumulative; each new disease attacked the weakened survivors of the last onslaught.

The tremendous impact of disease can be understood by considering population figures. In 1519, central Mexico had an Indian population estimated to have been 25 million. By 1523 only 17 million Indians survived; in 1548, only 6 million; in 1568, 3 million. By the early seventeenth century, the numbers of Indians of central Mexico scarcely reached 750,000; that is, only three percent of the population before the conquest.

Even if the estimate of the Indian population of central Mexico at the time of Cortés's landing is reduced by half, the effect of the conquest still has to be considered catastrophic. The decline would be from 12.5 million to 750,000—a fall of more than ninety percent in a century. For every sixteen Indians living when Cortés landed there would scarcely be one left a century later. This is a very conservative estimate.

It is estimated that the Indian population of Peru fell from 9 million before Columbus to 1.3 million by 1570. By the end of a half-century under Spanish rule, the populations of the peoples of the Aztec and Inca empires had undergone a devastating contraction.

In 1500 the population of the world was approximately 400 million, of whom 80 million (historian William H. McNeill puts it as high as 100 million) inhabited the Americas. By the middle of the century, of these 80 million, there remained only 10 million. This demographic disaster is without parallel. In the other continents—Africa and Asia—colonized by Europe, no similar population collapse occurred.

The new diseases travelled across the continents so swiftly that in some regions epidemics preceded the arrival of the Europeans by decades, even centuries. Often, when European invaders arrived, their Indian enemy was already weakened and demoralized by diseases against which they had no immunity and for which they had no remedy.

The *Chilam Balam,* a history of the Maya, written by Mayan scribes after the conquest, reflects the rupture that "the great dying" represented in Native history.

> There was then no sickness;
> they had no aching bone;
> they had then no fever;
> they had then no smallpox;
> they had then no burning chest;
> they had then no abdominal pain;
> they had then no consumption;
> they had then no headache;

> At that time the course of
> humanity was orderly.
> The foreigners made it otherwise
> when they arrived here.

These afflictions did more than reduce Indian populations to a fraction of their pre-conquest numbers. This unprecedented outbreak of disease not only decimated Indian populations, it also enfeebled the Indian will to resist. The loss of so many diminished the capacity of Indian societies to function. Leaders were dead, and whole generations of elders carrying the knowledge of the past were lost. Tradition gave way to expediency; Indian societies became immobilized and fragmented.

The conquest itself caused great demoralization among the Indians. This in turn produced a lassitude that made the Indians more susceptible to disease. Suicide was not uncommon. As the viceroy of Peru wrote: "The surrender that those who have been conquered have to make to the victor of self-esteem, wealth, prosperity, and comfort inevitably has repercussions on the raising of children, whom they can no longer afford to support." In early seventeenth-century New Granada (now Colombia), half the Indian families were childless. In the half that did have children, two was the most usual number, and a couple with as many as four was exceptional. The Native family shrank apace: abortion and infanticide became frequent. Their despair did not merely limit the Indians' desire to have children. Fr. Pedro de Córdoba wrote:

> The women worn out with labouring, have given up conceiving and bearing children, so that they will not expose themselves to the work piled upon work that is the lot of expectant or newly delivered mothers; their fear of the fatigue of child-bearing is so great that many of them, on finding themselves pregnant, have taken drugs so they will lose their babies, and have aborted them. And others, who have already given birth, kill their children with their own hands.

The Indians thought disease was connected with supernatural power; the Indians died from the onslaught of disease while the Spanish seemed unaffected. This led the Indians to accept the enthronement of the Spaniards and their god. The explanations of death that Indian culture could offer from its past could not encompass the disease and destruction that had been visited on them. Ceremonies of birth, marriage and death disappeared. Old customs died.

The epidemic diseases that have traversed the Americas over the last five hundred years have had a dramatic effect on the lives of Native people: the depopulation of large areas of the two continents; the reorganization of land and labour; and in many regions the disappearance of traditional political, social and religious structures.

McNeill says that, more than any other factor, disease allowed the Spaniards to transfer their culture and language to the New World, "making it normative even in regions where millions of Indians had previously lived according to customs and standards of their own."

The impact of disease was not confined to the Aztecs and the Incas, nor to the sixteenth and seventeenth centuries. It continued, decade after decade, century after century, until even the Indians of the most inaccessible regions succumbed.

In the Brazilian rainforest, the encroachment and spread of disease did not occur until the twentieth century; some of its tribes were falling ill for the first time in the 1950s. But these Indians of the rainforest were struck by the viruses and bacteria of four centuries of contact within a period of a few years. There were the epidemic killers of the conquest, smallpox and measles. There were the diseases of tropical Africa, malaria and yellow fever. And finally, there were the great twentieth-century killers, influenza and tuberculosis. When these diseases reached the rainforest, they overwhelmed unprotected tribal societies.

In 1898 Carl Ranke, a medical doctor who made a survey of the health of the tribes of the Xingú (a tributary of the Amazon), noted that among 800 to 1,000 Indians that he examined in the jungle he encountered fractures, some enteritis and a tumour; the only disease was malaria. But he was aware that the extraordinarily good health of the Indians was bound to deteriorate: "Poor people! It is already possible to predict their destiny . . . syphilis, leprosy, tuberculosis, measles, scarlet fever, smallpox, yellow fever and berri berri." At the time of Ranke's visit, there were between 3,000 and 4,000 Indians living in the Xingú basin. By 1952 there were only 652.

Influenza, which devastated the world in 1918–19, struck the

Amazon as well. It took five years to pass through the jungle, spreading from tribe to tribe along the great waterways and causing thousands of deaths along its route. Some of the tribes were swiftly wiped out.

Darcy Ribeiro, an anthropologist who went to help the Urubus-Kaapor in 1950, has written an account of a measles attack that killed 160 of a population of 750 people. By the time he arrived in the village only a few Indians still had the strength to put coats of palm leaves over their backs. Most of the inhabitants, prostrated by the disease, lay unconscious in the rain.

> [T]hey no longer had the strength to get to the extensive community gardens in order to get food, they could not even get water. They were dying as much from hunger and thirst as from the disease. Sick children crawled along the ground trying to keep the fires lit despite the rain, to keep themselves warm. Their fathers, burning with fever, could do nothing; the mothers, unconscious, pushed away the children who wanted to nurse at their breasts.

Thriving villages collapsed. Diseases halted food production. Men could not go into the forests in pursuit of game; the women could not cultivate their manioc gardens. An epidemic could be a sentence of death, not just for the sick but also for the enfeebled survivors left without food, water and wood.

By the 1950s the invasion of the Brazilian rainforest had begun in earnest; airstrips were being bulldozed in the jungle, miners, woodworkers and farm labourers were scouting for lands and resources. With them, they brought new diseases—tuberculosis and syphilis—that attacked Indian communities more slowly than the old plagues, but just as relentlessly. Depopulation placed enormous stress on the social institutions of Native society. The epidemics rent the fabric of Native culture.

From 1900 to 1957, according to Ribeiro, the Indian population of Brazil dropped from one million to less than 200,000. Seventy-eight Indian tribes became extinct.

In North America the same decimation of Indian populations occurred. Certainly the North American Indian population was much less at the time of first contact than that of Central and South America had been. But can we say with any assurance how many died? Two rival schools of thought have fuelled the debate. The American historical school, led by Alfred Kroeber, has argued that disease was just one of a number of factors that influenced the dramatic decline in population. This school says that the population of North American Indians before contact was one million; the decline after contact was moderate and not attributable to disease.

A group of ethnohistorians, led by Henry Dobyns, disputes this claim. Dobyns asserts that epidemics were decisive demographic events. He estimates the population of North America before the arrival of Columbus to have been more than 18 million, and a post-contact decline of 95 percent over 130 years. He concludes that only the devastation of repeated epidemics could account for a loss of this magnitude. Ann F. Ramenofsky has taken newly available data on population variations among North American Indian groups and subjected it to statistical scrutiny. Her conclusion bears out the thesis of a high population before Columbus (she estimates it at 10 million or more) and drastic post-contact decline.

In North America, Europeans looked upon the appalling losses among the Indian populations as providential. The depopulation of Native lands left large tracts available for colonization, to the satisfaction of many European immigrants. One Frenchman said that "it appears visibly that God wishes that they yield their place to new peoples."

Studies of the impact of the advent of Europeans in more recent times bear out the likelihood of a drastic and general decline in Indian numbers in North America owing to disease. In the 1890s, the American whaling fleet from San Francisco entered the Beaufort Sea and established whaling stations in the western Arctic. Eskimos were hired to gather driftwood to conserve the ships' stocks of coal, and to hunt caribou and muskox to supply the whalers with fresh meat. Whaling took a heavy toll of bowhead whales. But it was not just the animals that were affected by the coming of the whalers.

The whalers brought syphilis, measles and other diseases. When the whaling industry collapsed in 1908, of the original population of 2,500, there were only about 250 Mackenzie Eskimos left in the region between Barter Island and Bathurst Peninsula. This is why today most of the Inuvialuit, the Native people of Canada's western Arctic, are the descendants of Eskimos who immigrated to Canada from Alaska in the early years of this century.

We are inclined to think that these calamities no longer threaten the Native people of North America. To be sure, the old diseases may have been conquered, but now the impact of European domination takes other forms. These new social pathologies can be as devastating as the old diseases. In northern Canada, in recent years, public health services have been provided in even the most remote Native villages and camps. Improved medical services have not, however, solved Native peoples' health problems. Certainly, tuberculosis has been brought under control, and influenza, measles and whooping cough no longer cause many deaths. Nevertheless, in northern Canada Native people do not share the same measure of good health that other Canadians enjoy.

When I conducted the Mackenzie Valley Pipeline Inquiry I was given a picture of the impact of the advance of governmental and industrial activity in Canada's Arctic and sub-Arctic regions, in terms of its effect on physical and mental health. Doctors and nurses who had been active in the North for years described to the Inquiry the deterioration in the health of their Native patients. Native people eat less meat, more sugar, and mothers may be encouraged to bottle-feed rather than breast-feed their babies. Some changes are plain to see, such as the consumption of enormous quantities of soda pop. An epidemic of dental disease and high rates of tooth decay and gum disease are the outcome. A change in diet may cause such problems when we realize that traditional food, such as seal and caribou, has a higher dietary value than imported meats.

But the diseases that are creating the most serious problems for Native people have a social as well as a medical profile. The former causes of sickness have been replaced by new ones—less deadly, but nonetheless debilitating.

Doctors with wide experience in northern communities told the Inquiry that during the decade of the 1970s venereal disease rates rose rapidly in the Northwest Territories, attaining levels many times higher than those for Canada as a whole. Dr. Herbert Schwarz, testifying before the Inquiry, spoke of the rate of venereal disease in Inuvik, the regional centre for the Mackenzie Delta area:

Mr. Commissioner, if we apply these 1975 Inuvik percentages and figures for the seven-month period only showing that one person in every six was infected with gonorrhea, and transpose these figures on a per capita basis to a city like Ottawa, then [it] would have from 80,000 to 100,000 people suffering with venereal disease. [The] city would be a disaster area and a state of medical emergency proclaimed.

Then there is alcohol. Alcohol was apparently used by some of the Indians of the Americas before the advent of Europeans, but only among agricultural peoples, not among hunters and gatherers. Today the subjects of drinking and drunkenness recur in every discussion of social pathology in every Native community. Native people themselves regard the abuse of alcohol as the most disruptive force, the most alarming symptom and perhaps the most serious danger to the future of their communities. No one who travels in the Arctic and sub-Arctic can remain unaware of the social pathology that disfigures the life of Native communities—family violence, alcoholism and, saddest of all, suicide by young people, usually in their teens and early twenties. These lamentable statistics are the tragic outcome of the policies pursued by the dominant European society for many years.

Government policy has sought to bring industrial development to the northern frontier. Many isolated Native peoples must now confront the disruptive effects of the large-scale industrial development that is the norm in frontier regions. The values of White people working on the frontier are often opposed to and inconsistent with the values that are embedded in Native tradition in the villages and settlements of the North. The frontier ethos of European society encourages, indeed depends upon, a mobile if not footloose work force and all its ideological concomitants. It is not any particular location that matters but the profitability of an area; attachments are to material reward, not to place, people or community. Individualism, uncertainty and instability are part and parcel of the frontier, whether it be in the Arctic or the Amazon.

The community life of Native people, on the other hand, emphasizes sharing and cooperation between generations and among the member households of an extended family. The Native community has a profound sense of its own permanence. The shared place is more important than any economic incentive. Native people are well aware of the difference between their own values and those of a frontier work force. At Fort Good Hope, Agnes Edgi told the Inquiry:

> We, the Dene people, were born on this land of ours. We are not like the white people who go wandering around looking for work. They are not like us . . . who have a home in one place. They, the white people, move from one town to another, from one country to another, searching for jobs to make money.

The Native people believe that industrial advance affects the complex links between Native people and their past, between the generations, and between them and their culture. Economic forces imposed by European society can break these vital links. The more the industrial frontier displaces the Native homeland, the worse the incidence of crime and violence has been.

In the past, the representatives of powerful social and economic institutions in metropolitan Canada—government administrators, representatives of industry, missionaries and clergy, policemen, social workers and teachers, supplemented by invasions of physical and social scientists in season—were united in their dismissal of Native languages, cultures and traditions, and in their condemnation of ways of life different from their own. Natives were taught to reject their own people, their own past. The great river flowing into the Arctic, known to the Dene of the region as Deh-Cho, was renamed the Mackenzie River, after the Scotsman whom the Indians guided to its delta. Native students, inadequately educated to enter a White world that has too often been closed to them, feel cornered, frustrated and hostile. Frequently these feelings have erupted in violence, turned inward, against themselves.

Unfortunately, these causes are not treatable by a short stay in a detoxification centre, by counselling, or by any conventional means. They stem from individual demoralization and the demoralization of whole communities. It may be no exaggeration to speak at times of a despair that has overwhelmed whole villages.

Dr. Pat Abbott, a psychiatrist with the Division of Northern Medicine, Department of Health and Welfare, in his testimony to the Inquiry, made a point that is vital to understanding these problems. The establishment of new programs, the recruitment of personnel, the delivery of improved health services and social services by themselves are an exercise in futility. Abbott pointed out that psychiatry in the Arctic and sub-Arctic must take into account the cultural and social conditions of the people. He elaborated upon the difference between disorders that are individual, and therefore amenable to treatment at the individual level, and those that are social.

> The vast majority of the problems that I have seen as a clinical psychiatrist cannot, in all honesty, be classified as psychiatric problems. . . . many of the problems seen are so closely interwoven with the life-style of the Native people in the North, which in turn is closely bound to such problems as economics, housing, self-esteem and cultural identity, that to label them as psychiatric disorders is frankly fraudulent and of no value whatsoever, as the treatment must eventually be the treatment of the whole community rather than [of] the individual.

This was said in 1976, but I have never since heard it put better. We have tried to transform Native people. We told them to believe in our religion, not theirs. We told them to attend our schools, that they could learn nothing from their own people. We told them they must speak our languages, not theirs. We told them they must adopt the values of our culture, not theirs. So said—and still say—the soldiers, missionaries, traders, bureaucrats and industrialists who have occupied their lands and invaded their minds. It is this attitude that stands in the way of Native people, as they seek to build healthy communities. Native people are determined to find a distinct and contemporary identity in the world that has replaced their own. They feel the tremendous pull exerted by the mass culture of North America. But searching for their own identity, they continue to resist assimilation. They may be torn, but they believe they cannot repudiate their past. This tension between the claims made on them by two worlds lies at the root of the disorders which afflict them. Disease and demoralization in Native communities can only be defeated by allowing Indian people to rebuild their social matrix, to reconstruct their own reasons for living.

A history of disease and death permeates relations between Whites and Natives today. Down the long passageways of time the memories of fire and epidemic occurring and recurring, manifesting themselves today in marginalization and despair, form a chain, linking the past to the present. If we are ever to break that chain, or to forge durable links in a new, stronger and healthier one, we must be willing to come to grips with the past that we share with the Native people, a past of which we are hardly aware but which they know too well. The cure for the pathology afflicting Native communities lies in acknowledging this—such would be "the treatment of the whole community."

CHAPTER 4

Indian Slavery:
Brazil and the Carolinas

In May 1989, David Suzuki, the scientist and broadcaster, asked me to meet Paiakan Kayapó, leader of the Kayapó Indians of the Amazon, whom David had brought to Vancouver. Paiakan's tribe, dwelling far inland, was seeking support in its attempt to stop a hydro-electric project. The cause of the Indians of the Amazon has gained support worldwide. Scientists and rock stars support Paiakan's people and other endangered tribes of the Amazon. In a way, however, their cause is a sideshow. Concern with the rainforest is primarily environmental. We would be seeking to halt its destruction even if there were no Indians living along the great river and its tributaries. The dispute over the Brazilian rainforest has made us aware that Indian tribes living on the Amazon's upper reaches face an extraordinary challenge to their survival. But what about the fate of the Indians of Brazil in centuries past?

Because so much has been written about the conquest of the Aztec and Inca empires, we may forget that these epic adventures were only one of two processes of conquest and colonization. As the Spanish advanced along the spine of the Americas, from Mexico to Peru, other European nations were penetrating the lowlands along the Atlantic seaboard of North and South America. The Spanish had by means of a series of sharp military advances defeated the dynasties of the cordillera. Portuguese and English explorers had to work their way inland in a series of protracted guerilla wars.

In Mexico and in the Andes the Spaniards were generally dealing with settled Indian populations—they could force them to labour without enslaving them. In the Atlantic lowlands of the Americas, however, Portuguese and English settlers sought to establish a plantation economy. This agricultural mode had two requirements that profoundly affected Native people: it required the land to be cleared of its traditional inhabitants and it required a new form of labour—slavery.

It is a myth, still held by many, that there was no system of Indian slavery in the Americas. We think of the system of slavery that arose in the New World as one which enslaved only Africans. The Portuguese and the English, however, had earlier established Indian slavery, laying the foundations for the enslavement of millions of Africans by the two great slaveholding states of the New World, Brazil and the United States. In Brazil, the Portuguese developed an organized system of Indian slavery before they brought in Africans as slaves. Farther north, the English established an Indian slave trade, in what is now the southeastern United States, before they had imported African slaves to the region.

Both the Portuguese and English settlers relied heavily on slave traders who would venture into the forest and capture Indians to be sold into slavery. The result was bloodshed and butchery. Indians were slaughtered and others enslaved, flogged and required to submit to life at hard labour. By the end of the seventeenth century, when the coast of South America had been colonized from the Guianas to the Paraná, a million Indians had died. In the southeastern United States not one tribe remained in possession of its traditional lands; the English annihilated tribal peoples along the coast and for hundreds of kilometres inland.

Slavery was deeply rooted in the Mediterranean countries, in-

Rule of

Just war

cluding Spain. Historically in Europe, enemies captured in a just war could be enslaved, and persons already enslaved could be purchased and kept in slavery. Las Casas himself had not at first opposed African slavery, on the ground that the Africans had been captured in just wars. Europe had created an international market in which human beings were bought, sold and transported in bulk. When Columbus captured Indians and brought them back to Spain as slaves, he was simply following established precedents. But doubt arose over this justification: Columbus had entered the Caribbean and assaulted Indians defending their homes. Uncertainty led the Crown to sequester the proceeds of the sale of Columbus's slaves.

The Spanish Crown had trouble coming to any firm conclusions about slavery in the New World. Were the Indians incorrigibly hostile to Spain? If so, they could be enslaved. But were they hostile? Who could say? Could the Crown rely on the evidence of the slavers? In 1530 Madrid prohibited the enslavement of Indians whatever the pretext. But with the discovery of Peru, the prohibition was suspended for that country, then it was suspended for Guatemala, then for the whole of the Caribbean. In 1534 the Crown declared that all hostile Indians could be enslaved. As the Conquest proceeded, other causes were added as justification for enslaving the Indians: cannibalism, opposition to the Catholic faith, even simple resistance to the establishment of Spanish settlements. In 1537 Pope Paul III declared that no Christian could enslave an Indian on pain of excommunication, but this ruling was never enforced in the New World.

Ok to enslave

Not ENFORCED

By this time, however, the encomienda system had become entrenched. The Spaniards did have slaves, but the largest number of Indians were held in subjection by encomienda. In a sense it made no difference to the conquistadores: under encomienda they exercised virtually unlimited power over the Indians allotted to them. The debate in Spain about the legitimacy of slavery was in its own way fascinating, but the reality across the Atlantic was such that, to the Indians, the outcome hardly mattered.

It was not the Spanish but the Portuguese and the English who were to make the greatest use of slavery. Each established a commercial empire in Indian slaves.

Eng & Portuguese

In Brazil, the story of slavery is the story of techniques that the Portuguese developed to deprive the Indians of their liberty and their land: war, treachery and the deliberate exacerbation of con-

flicts between traditional tribal enemies. It is also the story of the development of an immense slave trade in which Portuguese traders,
settlers and members of the clergy travelled up the river valleys to
capture entire tribes of Indians. It is also the story of life in slavery:
Indians were beaten, put into stocks and worked to death.

The Portuguese divided the Indians of the Brazilian coast into two
groups: the Tupi and the Tapuya. Each of these designations, however, encompassed many Indian tribes. The Tupi predominated
along the Amazon and in the coastal area from the Amazon to the
Rio de la Plata. The Tupi tribesmen were the first Natives the Europeans encountered. They lived in small and temporary villages, each
often surrounded by a wooden stockade, usually located along a
river bank.

Wars were frequent between these Indians. As a result the Portuguese were to enjoy something like the advantages which had
enabled Cortés and Pisarro to achieve their stunning military suc-
cesses. The traditional enmities between the tribes facilitated the development of the Indian slave trade.

Cabral's accidental discovery of Brazil, in 1500, on a voyage to
Africa, became the foundation for Portugal's claims in the New
World. For the Portuguese, the immediate attraction of Brazil was
the Brazilwood tree, coveted as a source of purple dye in the manu-
facture of textiles. The work involved in cutting and transporting
the trees was physically punishing, and Indians were recruited for
the task. They were prepared to endure the arduous labour because
the Europeans rewarded them with trade goods. The Tupi tribes
along the coast were engaged in slash and burn agriculture which required the clearing of large areas of rainforest. Metal hoes and
scythes were invaluable for this work. Constructing a thatched-roof
house or a canoe were tasks that were measurably shortened by the
use of metal axes. Fishing was easier with metal hooks, and hunting
with steel knives.

The Portuguese, like the Spanish before them, were not eager to
do manual labour, preferring to have the Indians do it for them. The
Indians paddled the canoes that carried the Portuguese along the
rivers and they acted as domestic servants. But more important to
the incipient sugar economy, they planted, tended and harvested
their sugar cane. Sugar soon supplanted the Brazilwood trade as Brazil's main industry.

Brazil's first shipments of sugar to Europe began in the late 1530s. In 1549 Brazil became a royal colony. The arrival in Brazil in that year of Martin Afonso de Sousa as governor general, accompanied by members of the Jesuit order, together with a thousand colonists, marked the determination by the Crown to take colonization seriously. And in Brazil colonization meant sugar plantations. Brazil swiftly became pre-eminent in world production of sugar.

As the plantations expanded, the Indians could see that sugar threatened their continued existence. The Brazilwood trade had thinned the coastal rainforest, but the sugar plantations were causing a wholesale transformation of the coastal ecology. By the 1570s the forests of the coastal region, especially those around Rio de Janeiro and Salvador, as well as farther north at Recife, had been cleared and the land converted to sugar production. The rainforest all along the coast was eventually cut down. Seeing the rapid destruction of their land, the Tupinambá of the north coast rose up in sporadic revolts.

The Tupinambá uprisings provided the Portuguese with an excuse to enslave the Indians. Slaves could be captured in a just war, one sanctioned by the King as a reprisal against Indians who had attacked the Portuguese. In 1558, Mem de Sá, the third royal governor, decided to make war against the Indians, and to bring the survivors among them back as slaves.

This was a war entailing carnage of a different order of magnitude to that seen in skirmishes traditionally fought among tribal peoples along the coast. Many of the Portuguese rode on horseback, armed with swords and muskets. The Indian bows and arrows were no match for firearms and armour, no matter the number of Indian warriors. The Portuguese fought to destroy their enemy, taking lives and captives. After defeating the Tupinambá, the Portuguese armed them to serve as auxiliaries to the Portuguese conquerors, and undertook a campaign against the neighbouring Caeté, seizing thousands more as slaves.

With the defeat of the Caeté, the pattern of Portuguese enslavement of the Indians was fixed. The labour supply required for the sugar plantations would be acquired by sending expeditions into Indian territory to take Indians as captives. The land thus emptied of its population would be turned over to settlers to grow sugar and to raise cattle.

By 1600 Brazil was supplying almost all of Europe's sugar. The expansion of the Brazilian economy and the king's revenues depended on the sugar plantations and they in turn depended on slave labour. The system of slave-hunting and slavery became entrenched at all levels of Brazilian society. The slaving that had at first provided labour for the plantation economy came to provide labour for the cattle ranches and the mines. By the end of the sixteenth century, land had been cleared for settlement along the entire eastern seaboard. A little more than a century later, cattle were being raised deep in the interior.

Farther south, from São Paulo, private expeditions were organized to search for slaves. These expeditions were known as *bandeiras*. Settlers would hire mercenaries to lead parties of friendly Indians along the great waterways leading into the interior. For one hundred and fifty years the Portuguese annually dispatched flotillas of canoes into the interior, where they would take entire villages into slavery. The expeditions, which often included settlers, mercenaries, missionaries and thousands of Indians, would use persuasion and, if that did not work, violence to entrap Indians. A priest who witnessed some of the early bandeiras wrote:

> . . . they razed and burned entire villages, which are generally made of dry palm leaves, roasting alive in them those that refused to surrender as slaves. They overcame and subjugated others peacefully, but by execrable deceit. They would promise them alliances and friendship in the name and good faith of the King. But once they had them off guard and unarmed, they seized and bound them all, dividing them among themselves as slaves or selling them with the greatest cruelty.

Such slaving expeditions might take several years and cover thousands of kilometres. One of the longest involved a journey of 11,000 kilometres from São Paulo to the Madeira River, and then down the Amazon to the coast.

For the Indians brought to the slave markets of the coast, life was frightful. Families were broken up during the raids, and a large proportion of the men were killed. The women and children were taken down river in chains and sold. On the sugar plantations, they were forced to work seven days a week. The work was punishing. It required clearing and irrigating huge tracts of land, building mills, houses and roads, and cutting and pressing the cane. Like the Indians who were subjugated by the Spanish, the Indians of Brazil, by virtue of enforced labour and the onslaught of disease, suffered greatly. Not many survived. So, the planters turned to Africa. A forced migration of millions of Africans began in the mid-sixteenth century and continued until 1850.

Brazil had the greatest number of African slaves of any country of the New World. At least 3.5 million African slaves were imported. But it is very likely that Brazil also had the greatest number of Indian slaves of any country of the New World. Some estimate that the bandeiras may have furnished Brazil with 350,000 Indian slaves in this period. Hundreds of thousands more were killed. Historian John Hemming estimates that the Native population of the Amazon basin may have stood at something like 2.5 million before Cabral; it is no more than 100,000 today.

Portugal, like Spain, was a Catholic country. What of the Crown, eager to see the Indians brought under Portuguese rule as Christianized subjects, and theoretically loth to permit their enslavement? What of the Church, which had sent the Jesuits to Brazil?

Only 128 Jesuits arrived in Brazil between 1549 and 1598, but their impact was enormous. They intended to Christianize the Indians. Appalled by the cruelty of the Portuguese towards the Indians, the Jesuits sought to protect the Indians by gathering them into farming communities, and establishing a network of villages under Jesuit protection, as Las Casas had tried to do in Guatemala.

Like Las Casas, the Jesuits took the Indians' case directly to the king to whom they reported the atrocities committed by the settlers. The planters sent their own representatives to court, who spoke of the Indians as barbarians. It was a reprise of the debate between Las Casas and Sepúlveda at Valladolid. In 1694, Domingos Jorge Velho summarized the planters' point of view in a submission to the king:

> And if we subsequently use them for our tillage and husbandry, we do them no injustice; for this is done as much to support them and their children as to support us and ours. This is so different from enslaving them that it is rather doing them

a priceless service, since we teach them to till, to sow, to reap, and to work for their keep—something which they did not know how to do before the whites taught them.

The kings of Portugal understood that the Indians were human beings. In his instructions to the first governor general of Brazil, King João III called for tolerance, understanding and forgiveness toward the Indians. But these pious expressions were of no consequence as long as the Portuguese could engage in just wars to obtain Indian slaves. In 1610 King Philip III declared that all Indians, whether Christian or heathen, were by nature free, could not be forced to work, and must be paid for their work when they volunteered it. In 1611, however, following settler riots in Brazil, he agreed to permit the enslavement of Indian prisoners taken in war.

Like Charles V of Spain, the kings of Portugal found that their unruly colonial subjects would not submit to laws that impeded their exploitation of Indian labour by force. In the end, it was the high death rate among the Indians, their retreat into the interior, and the importation of Africans that put an end to Indian slavery. The kings of Portugal, despite their high-minded declarations, had been as powerless to safeguard the rights and well-being of the Indians of Brazil as the kings of Spain had been in Mexico and Peru.

The colonies of the Spanish and the Portuguese were established decades before the English were to establish the colony of Virginia on the mainland of North America. By that time the Spanish had already laid claim to Florida by establishing a fort and a mission at St. Augustine.

In the meantime, in Brazil, African slavery was replacing Indian slavery. African slavery had also become entrenched in the Caribbean, where the English had a thriving colony, based on sugar, on the island of Barbados. African slavery had been formally established in Barbados in 1636, at first to provide labour for the cotton plantations. But links between Brazil and Barbados brought sugar to Barbados, and cane replaced cotton. The colony's plantation economy was based on slavery; indeed, it had made Barbados England's richest colony in the New World. So the English were already engaged in the enslavement of Africans. But they had not thus far engaged in the enslavement of Indians.

After Virginia, the English established colonies along the Atlantic seaboard. Except in the Carolinas, none of these colonies depended on Indian slavery. In the Carolinas, however, the English established a colony founded on Indian slavery. They started by enslaving the Indians on the Atlantic coast. As the demand for slaves increased, slaving parties ranged inland along the rivers, abducting Indians from villages as far away as the Mississippi. These incursions in search of slaves culminated in two great Indian rebellions. Settlers in North Carolina had to do battle with an alliance of Indian tribes in the Tuscarora War, and settlers in South Carolina in the Yamassee War. These wars pressed hard on the settlements in the Carolinas, almost bringing a complete halt to English colonization south of Virginia.

The first permanent English settlement in North America was established in 1607, at Jamestown, under the auspices of the Virginia Company. Jamestown was founded on land that belonged to the Powhatan Indians. The Powhatans were not at first concerned about the fledgling colony of Europeans. But the soil of Virginia proved to be ideal for growing tobacco, and more settlers came, more land came under cultivation, and the tobacco crop expanded.

The English, intending to drive the Indians off their land, cut down their corn and burned their villages. The Indians retaliated; their assaults on the colonists are known in conventional histories as the "massacres" of 1622 and 1644. Thereafter the Virginians feared and hated the Indians.

Indians were not enslaved to work on the plantations. Nevertheless, Virginia's traders were engaged in purchasing Indian slaves from tribes outside the colony, and selling them on the slave market.

The heart of the English slave trade was, however, in the Carolinas. In 1663 a group of royal favourites under Charles II received a proprietary grant of the Carolinas; it gave them the right not only to vast tracts of land in the country south of Virginia, but also a monopoly over trade in deer skins. Deer were plentiful, and deerskin much sought after in Europe. "There is such infinite Herds," wrote one of the settlers, "that the whole country seems but one continued Park."

The trade in deer skins grew rapidly. Charleston was established in 1670 and became the centre of the new colony. Here for the first time we encounter the fur trade, a commercial relationship wherein the Europeans and the Indians were in effect partners. The fur trade was even more important farther north; in Canada a nation was to be built on it.

The London proprietors recruited many settlers from Barbados, where African slavery was already entrenched. These settlers from Barbados transformed the economy of the Carolinas, and relations with the Indians as well. At first the settlers sought to grow sugar, citrus, cotton, tobacco and other crops, but with no marked success. They decided, therefore, that trade in Indians would be more profitable. Indians could be sold to work on sugar plantations of the West Indies. In the Carolinas, the English, for the first time in North America, launched raids on Indian tribes, not in defence of their settlements, not to obtain new land or a labour force for the land, but to gather them as slaves, as merchandise. The Indian slave trade became the cornerstone of commerce for the Charleston merchants.

In the Carolinas, the tension between the metropolitan centre and settlers on the frontier that the Portuguese and Spanish kings had faced with their wilful colonists was replicated. In England the proprietors of the colony were opposed to the development of Indian slavery. They needed to rely on their Indian trading partners to supply them with furs; they could not afford the disruption of an Indian war.

To protect their interests the London proprietors appointed a governor, but he was ignored by the settlers, who took the land they wanted without being concerned about the proprietors' plans. Nor were they willing to curtail their pursuit of Indian slaves.

In the late 1670s, the controversy between London and the settlers came to a head. The London proprietors claimed the loyalty of the Westos, one of the largest tribes in the Carolinas. The settlers armed another tribe, the Savannahs, and the Savannahs made war against the Westos. This war lasted three years, ending with the triumph of the Savannahs and the loss of the Westo population to slavery or death. The London proprietors claimed that the settlers had been able to recruit their Indian allies in the campaign to destroy the Westos, on account of the Savannahs' "covetousness of your guns Powder and Shott and other European Commodities." The settlers were now in the ascendancy, and the development of a full-scale slave trade was assured. By the end of the seventeenth century the

Carolina slave traders in search of Indian captives travelled hundreds of kilometres into the interior and south into Spanish Florida.

In 1704 James Moore of South Carolina led perhaps the most devastating raid ever made against the Indians. Setting out with fifty Whites and one thousand Indian mercenaries, he travelled across Georgia into Florida, destroying thirteen Spanish missions, killing several hundred Indians, and enslaving 325 Indian men, women and children.

At the beginning of the eighteenth century, a new crop, rice, well suited to the Carolina lowlands, was developed as a staple export. The demand for Indian land and Indian labour intensified. When the Savannahs, who had decimated the Westos, tried to migrate beyond the influence of the slavers, the merchants and traders at Charleston hired the Catawbas to slaughter them, to achieve the necessary "thinning out of the barbarous Indian native." By 1710, the Savannahs were virtually extinct.

The Indian slave trade in the Carolinas had many of the features of the Indian slave trade in Brazil. The settlers made alliances with Indian tribes on the coast. The settlers had what the Indians wanted: trade goods—metal knives, cooking utensils, fabrics. Gary B. Nash has written that the critical factor in White-Indian relations was the appetite of the Indians for trade goods. Furthermore, as Nash says, "the Indian desire for trade goods was so strong that nothing could deter new tribes from forging alliances with the colonizers while others were being destroyed." And the settlers were able to arm their Indian allies with guns. Indians, led by White mercenaries, raided other tribes farther inland. The striking feature of Indian slavery in the Carolinas is that it was not simply for the purpose of obtaining enforced labour for the nascent plantation economy, but rather for the purpose of exporting Indian slaves to slave economies overseas. Slaves were brought back to the coast, sold in Charleston and sent by ship mostly to the West Indies, though some were shipped to New York and New England.

Of all Indian tribes, it was the Tuscaroras who fell under the greatest threat of enslavement by the English. Living in villages in North Carolina, they were constantly under attack by slavers. In 1711, with new plantations being established on their territory, the Tuscaroras struck back. They made alliances with other tribes with similar grievances and fell on the European invaders. About one hundred and fifty settlers were killed in the initial attack. North Carolina, only thinly populated, turned to neighbouring colonies for help against the Indian attackers. The slave traders of South Carolina rode to the rescue. John Barnwell, one of the leading merchants in the South Carolina Indian trade, led a force of thirty-three White men and five hundred Yamassees into Tuscarora country. Barnwell engaged the Tuscaroras in a series of inconclusive skirmishes. A truce was reached with the Indians. But when Barnwell and his men violated the truce by seizing Indians and taking them as slaves to South Carolina, the Tuscaroras resumed their attacks on the settlers.

It was James Moore who mounted a second expedition against the Tuscaroras. He recruited an army composed of thirty-three White men (oddly enough, the same number as Barnwell had recruited) and nearly one thousand Cherokees, Yamassees, Creeks and Catawbas. On 25 March 1713 they won a "glorious victory" when they stormed the Tuscarora fort at Nooherooka. Moore's losses were not great. As for the Tuscaroras: "Enemies Destroyed is as follows—Prisoners 392, Scalps 192, out of ye sd. fort—and att. least 200 kill'd and Burnt in ye fort—and 166 kill'd and taken out of ye fort." As many as four hundred survivors, mostly women and children, were led back to the Charleston slave market. The remnants of the tribe travelled northward in the aftermath of the war, migrating to New York to obtain shelter under the wing of the Iroquois, to become the sixth nation of the Iroquois Confederacy.

Two years after the Yamassees had participated in the defeat and enslavement of the Tuscaroras, they themselves, unwilling to be impressed into plantation slavery, rose in rebellion. It was the most successful resistance movement in the history of the southern colonies, an uprising that included not only many of the coastal tribes but also one of the interior tribes, the Creeks. In the Yamassee War the Indians came as close as the Indians were ever to come in British North America in the colonial period to overwhelming the Europeans.

The Yamassee attack on Good Friday in 1715 was carefully co-ordinated with the Creeks. One of the most powerful interior tribes, the Creeks were incited to join in the attack by the French, who had been building forts and trading posts in the Mississippi Valley and were trying to turn the Creeks against the English. When the

Yamassees and the Creeks attacked in force, it created havoc in South Carolina. During the summer of 1715 Charleston quickly filled up with refugee colonists. The colonists mounted counterattacks on the Yamassees, but the Yamassees' allies, the Creeks, were still razing English settlements. Moreover, the Creeks were negotiating with the Cherokees, the largest Indian nation neighbouring the southern colonies, to join the rebellion.

But the Cherokees were dependent on English trade goods; in the end this dissuaded them from joining in the uprising. As they told the Carolinians, unless they were at war with the Creeks "they should have no way in getting of Slaves to buy ammunition and clothing" from the White traders. Once again, the Indians' paramount concern with access to European trade goods made all the difference. With the decision of the Cherokees to ally themselves with the colonists, the Yamassee War was over. The Creeks retreated to the interior, beyond the Savannah River, and the Yamassee retreated to Florida. The plantation economy soon occupied the coastal land and cattle ranches were established in the interior. In 1732 the king granted to James Oglethorpe land beyond the Savannah River, which became the colony of Georgia.

In the Carolinas the English settlers' relentless exploitation of Indian labour and trade in Indian people was unrestrained by the remonstrances of church or state. Despite the cruelty of their policy the English were able to enlist the Indian tribes to enslave one another and, in the Tuscarora and Yamassee Wars, to keep them in diplomatic disarray at a time when united Indian support of the uprising might have routed English settlement in the region. Despite the devastating toll that slave raiding took on their people, the tribes of the Carolinas were not able to unite against those who held the cornucopia that yielded guns, knives, utensils, sugar and coffee.

Nobody knows how many Indian slaves were taken in the Carolina slave trade. Historian Charles Hudson has said that Indian slavery "assumed far greater proportions than people today realize." In 1708, when the total population of South Carolina was 9,580, including 2,900 Blacks, there were also 1,400 Indian slaves, including five hundred men, six hundred women and three hundred children. We do know that all of the tribes that had occupied land in the southeastern United States were killed, enslaved, driven into the interior, or escaped to remote areas of Florida. Those who survived enslavement were presumably absorbed among the Blacks in subsequent generations.

The English were not troubled by the profound questions that had been debated at Valladolid. They were Protestants, not Catholics; they were under no obligation to Christianize the Indians. Not for them the conundrum presented to the Spanish and the Portuguese by the need, for economic purposes, to subjugate and enslave the Indians and at the same time to Christianize them and to acknowledge their humanity.

The Spanish enterprise in the New World was an imperial one, on behalf of and under the direction of Madrid. So also in the case of Portugal. But the English colonists were entrepreneurs. They had a free hand in dealing with the Indians. Not until the Royal Proclamation of 1763 did the government in London lay down a comprehensive policy, applicable throughout North America, designed to protect the Indians.

If the English were animated by an idea, it was the idea of progress, which was realized by the pioneer's relentless movement across the Atlantic and across North America. Commanded by God to subdue the earth, the English and then the Americans believed they had a mandate to conquer the wilderness. It was not a wilderness, of course, for it supported many human cultures. But for the colonists, Indians and their works did not qualify as human. In the minds of the English, the Indians living in the midst of the wilderness had to be subdued along with it.

To the English the Indians were proof of man's ascent from savagery to civilization. The Indians were what the Europeans once had been. The only measurement, the only standard by which to judge them was that of Europe. Romantic notions may have existed of the Noble Savage, but insofar as he was noble, the savage was so because he was child-like. Insofar as he was savage, he was morally and intellectually deformed. As a consequence, the Indians were not truly human.

The Europeans who came to the Americas organized their relations with the Indians in three ways: there was the encomienda system, there was the fur trade, and there was slavery. By comparing these three systems of economic exploitation and their consequences, the true horror of slavery becomes evident.

In the highlands of the cordillera, in the highly organized empires of the Aztecs and the Incas, the Spanish used the encomienda to transfer power over land and labour to the Spaniards. Even allowing for the devastating impact of war and disease, this system left the Indian agricultural communities largely intact.

The trade in deer skins in the Carolinas resembled the trade in fur that was the pattern farther north. The colony of New France on the St. Lawrence was established to trade in furs; its success depended on amicable relations with the Indians, on the Indians staying on the land to gather furs. This established the initial pattern, at least, of White-Indian relations in Canada.

Indian slavery, however, utterly destroyed the Indian way of life. The Portuguese in Brazil and the English in the Carolinas required control over the land and Indian slaves to develop crops that were new to the region even though it meant compelling the forced labour of Indians who had never before engaged in large-scale agriculture.

Not surprisingly, the three modes of economic exploitation have forced twentieth-century Natives to adopt different strategies for redressing the wrongs of the past. Many of the Indian tribes who became partners in the fur trade are fighting in the courts to secure their right to land and to fish and wildlife harvests. The Indians of the highlands are pressing their governments for agrarian reform legislation—not individual or community title alone, but a wholesale restructuring of the land base from Mexico to Chile. But the Indians of the Atlantic seaboard in North and South America are for the most part silent, the victims of a system of slavery that killed, absorbed or expelled them within two centuries of contact.

CHAPTER 5

Indians as Allies: The Iroquois

Canadians were startled and anxious, during the summer of 1990, to see armed Iroquois warriors at Oka, outside Montreal, standing off the Quebec police and the Canadian army to defend traditional ground that the local municipality had acquired in order to expand the local golf course. At the same time the Iroquois at Kahnawake put up barricades on their reserve opposite the island of Montreal, denying thousands of people, including the residents of suburban Chateauguay, access to the city. These were Mohawks, one of the Six Nations, the remnant of an Indian military power that once occupied the territory between New England and Quebec, between the English and the French colonists. Although today the Iroquois are reduced to a handful of reserves on the St. Lawrence and the Great Lakes, on both sides of the United States-Canada boundary, in the seventeenth, eighteenth and nineteenth centuries the European powers sought them as military allies.

The Spanish made use of Indian tribes as allies to topple the Aztec and Inca empires. But in North America, wherever their interests were in conflict, the English and the French sought the Indians as allies in their wars with each other. Of all the Indian nations, the Iroquois were the most important in a military sense, not only to the English, but also to the French, and later to the Americans, and finally to the Canadians.

The Spaniards had encountered two great Indian empires in the highlands of the cordillera. The Portuguese had encountered small tribes along the Atlantic lowlands. In the northeastern woodlands, the English and the French encountered an Indian political confederacy whose capacity for warfare extended far beyond its tribal territories.

John Cabot, a Venetian in English service, had sailed around Newfoundland in 1497, and English claims in North America were based on his discoveries. After a reconnaissance of the Gulf of St. Lawrence, a Frenchman, Jacques Cartier, in 1535, sailed up the St. Lawrence River to the then impassable rapids near present-day Montreal. He and his men wintered near present-day Quebec City. There they suffered severely from scurvy, and from the winter's cold, which they had not expected—Quebec City is just south of the latitude of Paris. Cartier thought he had found gold along the St. Lawrence for, like the Spaniards whose triumphs were fresh in European minds, he sought the precious metal. When he returned to France and his cargo turned out to be "fool's gold," interest in the St. Lawrence waned for more than half a century. Only towards the end of the sixteenth century, when beaver hats became fashionable in Europe, did the growing demand for beaver pelts encourage the French to sail along the shores of the Gulf of St. Lawrence and up the river itself to trade with Indians for furs.

In much of North America, especially in what is now Canada, the Europeans at first had no intention of settling the country. They cared only that fur was abundant and could be marketed in Europe. The fur trade was a partnership between European traders and the Indians who, as hunters and trappers, gathered the furs. In Mexico and Peru, the Spanish wanted Indian land and Indian labour. In northeastern North America the English and the French needed Indian labour, not Indian land, as long as their rivalry focused on the fur trade.

In 1608, with the founding of a settlement at Quebec, French activities in North America became centred on the St. Lawrence River, which offered access to a vast hinterland of fur. The French established a network of canoe routes which extended westward to the head of Lake Superior, and southward along the Ohio and the Mississippi, to trade with the Indians.

Occupying land in what is now the state of New York, the Iroquois were placed at the centre of conflict between the French on the St. Lawrence and the English along the Atlantic seaboard. Their land was not sought for plantation crops; New York was not subtropical like the middle Atlantic seaboard. Nor was Iroquois land sought for farming, at least not at first.

Throughout the seventeenth century and for the first half of the eighteenth century Britain and France were almost continuously at war. Every clash between the two powers was carried into North America. Indeed, relations between the French and the English in North America often seem to have been a history of meaningless wars with confusing names and obscure European origins.

When France and England exported their rivalries and wars from Europe to the New World they sought to ally the Indians with their respective causes. Why? Because the Indian nations were seasoned military powers, used to fighting in the North American territories. The most powerful of the northeastern tribes was the Iroquois. Their sphere of influence extended from the Atlantic to the Mississippi and from the St. Lawrence to the Ohio River and beyond.

The Iroquois were not passive observers of these struggles between the European powers, not helpless bystanders watching foreign armies tramping back and forth across their territory. They were a formidable nation, armed and organized. They chose sides, and in doing so were guided by what they conceived to be their own best interests. These shifting Iroquois alliances were not whimsical: at all times they sought to defend their sovereignty and their land.

Fundamentally, the Iroquois understood these quarrels to be about land—*their* land, *their* ancient territories—and they were determined to protect what was theirs. From time to time, they collaborated with both the English and the French, and with both the Canadians and the Americans.

The Iroquois did more than wage war; they were traders who travelled the paths that linked Indian nations together across most of eastern North America. The Iroquois language was the language of diplomacy among Indians along much of the English colonial frontier. In fact, during the summer of 1990, representatives of the Iroquois Confederacy came to Montreal to negotiate on behalf of the Mohawks in an attempt to bring a peaceful end to the confrontation between the Mohawk warriors at Oka and the Canadian army.

'Iroquois' is a term designating a confederacy of Indian nations, known to Europeans as the League of the Iroquois or the Iroquois Confederacy. At first the Confederacy consisted of the Seneca, Cayuga, Oneida, Onondaga and Mohawk nations. When the Tuscarora were driven from the Carolinas, they migrated northward; the five nations became the Six Nations. Iroquois territory comprised a large part of what is now New York state, from the Adirondack Mountains to the Great Lakes and from Lake Ontario to Pennsylvania. The Iroquois were agriculturalists, living in stockaded towns or villages. The people lived in longhouses; several families might live in one such dwelling. Villages might have a few small longhouses or as many as fifty. The Iroquois used the metaphor of the Longhouse to describe their confederacy; the Seneca, as the most westerly tribe, were known as "keepers of the western door," and the Mohawk as "keepers of the eastern door." At the time of contact the Iroquois numbered 10,000 to 15,000. Some put the figure higher, at 20,000 to 30,000.

The Iroquois were typical of the Indian tribes of North America in their belief in communal ownership of property. "No hospitals [poorhouses] are needed among them," wrote a French Jesuit in 1657, "because there are neither mendicants nor paupers as long as there are any rich people among them. Their kindness, humanity, and courtesy not only makes them liberal with what they have, but causes them to possess hardly anything except in common. A whole village must be without corn, before any individual can be obliged to endure privation." These values were shared by virtually all the Indian peoples of North America.

What was unique to the Iroquois was their form of political organization. It was not a centralized empire like that of the Aztecs or the Incas. Instead, it was a vast extension of the kinship groups that characterized the structure of political organization among the Indians of the eastern woodlands. The Iroquois family was matrilineal, with family membership determined through the female line. In turn, several matrilineal kinship groups might be grouped together in clans. A village might have a dozen or more clans. Each village and each nation were governed by their own councils. Villages combined to create a nation; the nations combined to form the confederacy. The confederacy was governed by a council of fifty leaders.

Within the Confederacy the sovereignty of each member nation was respected. The confederacy, established at least a century before the Europeans entered Iroquois territory for mutual protection and defence, was itself empowered to act for all the Iroquois. The Europeans, especially the English, were undoubtedly impressed by its sophistication. Bruce Johansen, in *Forgotten Founders,* has gone so far as to suggest that federalism was not invented by the Founding Fathers of the United States at Philadelphia in 1787—it had its genesis in the principles of the Iroquois Confederacy. This is not an idiosyncratic view. Many historians, including Henry Steele Commager, have acknowledged the contribution of Iroquois ideas to the political thought of the Founding Fathers, especially Benjamin Franklin.

The Iroquois also made an impression on Friedrich Engels. Engels was struck by the Confederacy's ability to maintain social cohesion without an elaborate state apparatus. The Iroquois, wrote Engels, provided an example of a living society that "knows no state." Engels' view was ethnocentric; in the Six Nations, the state may not have withered away, as Engels supposed, but then it had never achieved European proportions in terms of its authority over the life of its people. There were well-established forms of political organization among the Iroquois, but, unlike the political institutions of the Aztecs or the Incas, they bore no resemblance to the European state; certainly there was no authority resembling the monarchs of Europe and the central authorities governing in their names. There was no easy correlation with the relationship in Europe between state and subject.

When I was in school we were not told of the sophistication of the Iroquois Confederacy, but rather of the Iroquois' fierce attacks on the Hurons and the French priests who lived among them. The Iroquois and the Huron were indeed mortal enemies. In 1649, Iroquois warriors attacked the Hurons and killed every one they could find. They captured the Jesuit Fathers Brébeuf and Lalemant and tortured them to death. The remnant of the Huron, barely five hundred in number, made their way to Quebec. Now the Iroquois and the French were to remain enemies for half a century.

The Iroquois were in a strong position in the fur trade, acting as middlemen for the western tribes of the Great Lakes region. They preferred to sell their fur at Albany, where the English offered higher prices than the French and a wider range of trade goods. New France was a colony with only one-twentieth the population of the English settlements on the Atlantic coast. The lands controlled by the Iroquois were the greatest obstacle to its expansion.

The principal struggle, therefore, in the seventeenth century was between the Iroquois and the French. The French, feeling they had to interrupt the flow of fur to Albany, launched attacks on Iroquois villages. The Iroquois retaliated with swift and terrifying raids upon the French, ambushes from forest cover on unsuspecting encampments or travelling parties. By such means the Iroquois demonstrated that they could check the advance of French settlement. At their height the Iroquois raids almost overwhelmed the struggling French outposts. One Iroquois chief boasted, "[the French] were not able to goe over a door to pisse." Their attacks on the French in 1660 at the Long Sault and in 1689 at Lachine were devastating setbacks for the French; for a time the French considered abandoning New France.

By the end of the seventeenth century, however, both the Iroquois and the French were weary of war, and ready to make peace. At the same time the English sought an alliance with the Iroquois. The French advance south from the St. Lawrence Valley and north from Louisiana threatened to confine the English to the Atlantic seaboard.

In 1701 the Iroquois made a sudden peace with both the French and the English, signing treaties at Albany and Montreal which became known as the 'covenant chain'. As historian J. R. Miller has written,

> The Iroquois strategy was easily understood; given their vulnerable location, and given their exhaustion from the protracted struggle with the French . . . it made perfect sense for them to try to sit out the wars and to profit as much as they could from the European rivalries that lay behind them.

By these treaties the Iroquois intended to preserve their sovereignty. They never did regard themselves as subjects of either England or France. They were allies, not dependents, and they remained a formidable power. In 1711, the governor of Quebec wrote that it would be wise to avoid war with the Iroquois, since "the five Iroquois [nations] are more to be feared than the English colonies."

The covenant chain served the Iroquois well for half a century. They remained neutral and managed to stay aloof from the continual wars between the British and the French. In the long run the British were a greater threat to the Iroquois than the French. New France's primary interest was fur, not land, whereas the British colonies were constantly seeking to extend the agricultural frontier. But William Johnson, Britain's superintendent of Indian Affairs, married to a Mohawk woman, was able to bind the Mohawks, and to a lesser extent the other Iroquois nations, to the British. This was the situation at mid-century as the final war for supremacy in North America between the British and the French was about to take place.

In 1753, as war between Great Britain and France neared, the Mohawks, keepers of the eastern door, finding themselves in the way of the advance of English settlement, became incensed by the encroachment of settlers onto Iroquois territory and advised the British that they regarded the covenant chain as having been broken. In London, the Lords of Trade ordered the governor of New York to do all he could to restore amicable relations with the Iroquois. The result was the Albany Conference of 1754, which was called "to investigate and, if possible, to satisfy the Indians' complaints about fraudulent purchases and grants." The conference determined that all future purchases of land would have to be made "from the Indians in a body in their public Councils." This policy, designed to protect Indian lands, was to culminate in adoption of the Royal Proclamation of 1763.

War came in 1756. European historians called it the Seven Years' War; the Americans called it the French and Indian War. It was a struggle that saw the Indians align themselves with the French against the British and their colonies. The Indians and French in the interior defeated both British and American troops who were sent into the region. In 1754 Lieutenant-Colonel George Washington and his militiamen were expelled from the Ohio valley. British forces under Braddock were beaten the next year by a combined French and Indian force.

The British lost the early battles in North America to the French and the Indians, but the Royal Navy was able to stop the flow of supplies across the Atlantic from France. The French were forced to withdraw to their redoubt on the St. Lawrence. There, in 1759, the British and French fought the decisive battle on the Plains of Abraham, and Quebec was taken. The next year Montreal fell. By the Treaty of Paris in 1763, France relinquished virtually all of her claims to New France. All that remained of France's empire in North America were the small islands of St. Pierre and Miquelon and the French shore of Newfoundland.

The Iroquois were officially neutral during the Seven Years' War. An exception was the Mohawks, who fought alongside the English. In 1759, as it became apparent that Britain was likely to prevail, the Iroquois joined the British side.

In 1763 the British, by royal proclamation, provided for the reorganization of their North American possessions. For the Indians the significance of the Royal Proclamation of 1763 was enormous. The Proclamation was intended to avoid conflict between the Indians and land-hungry settlers. The first and fundamental principle of the Proclamation—which would offer greater protection to Indian land than any other single measure—was that Indian land could not be sold except to the Crown. The Indian hinterland, beyond the established colonies, was to be closed to agricultural expansion.

The Proclamation was to have profound implications, both immediately and throughout American and Canadian history. In the name of King George III, it provided that, it being

> essential to our Interest, and the Security of our Colonies, that the several Nations or Tribes of Indians with whom We are connected, and who live under our Protection, should not be molested or disturbed in the Possession of such Parts of Our Dominions and Territories as . . . are reserved to them, or any of them, as their Hunting Grounds . . . therefore . . . any Lands whatever, which, not having been ceded to or purchased by Us as aforesaid, are reserved to the said Indians. . . . And we do hereby strictly forbid, on Pain of our Displeasure, all our loving Subjects from making any Purchases or Settlements whatever,

or taking Possession of any of the Lands above reserved, without our especial leave and Licence for that Purpose first obtained.

All settlement had to stop at the crest of the Appalachians. Lands beyond this "Proclamation Line" were set aside for the Indians.

This had the effect of placing the British in precisely the position that the French had been, that is, resisting the advance of settlers from the Thirteen Colonies onto the lands of the interior Indians. And, like the French before them, it would lead them into conflict with their subjects in the Thirteen Colonies. Fur traders, land speculators and ordinary settlers were outraged by the Royal Proclamation of 1763. After all, the war with the French and the Indians had been fought to open up the lands beyond the Appalachians. Now Great Britain was closing off these same lands, just as the French had done.

The British policy exemplified by the Proclamation was one of the "Intolerable Acts" used to justify the American War of Independence. Indeed, the Americans accused the British of inciting the Indians to make war on them. The Declaration of Independence charged that the British king "has excited domestic insurrection among us, and has endeavoured to bring on the inhabitants of our frontiers, the merciless Indian Savages, whose known rule of warfare, is an undistinguished destruction of all ages, sexes, and conditions."

In the long term the Proclamation would have other profound implications. It would, after the British had retired from North America, and two new nation-states, the United States and Canada, had been established, be instrumental in the recognition by the courts of both countries of the distinctive political status and aboriginal rights of the Indians.

The Confederacy did not function as a unit during the American Revolutionary War. The six nations acted independently. Nevertheless, except for the Oneida, who fought on the side of the Americans, the Iroquois supported the British. They calculated that their interests would be better served if the British won than if the colonies, whence the American settlers came, were to be successful. During the war the Iroquois attacked and burned American forts and settlements on the New York and Pennsylvania frontiers. In retaliation the Americans invaded the Iroquois territories, destroying crops and burning their villages. The Iroquois term for General George Washington was "town-destroyer," after the ruthless manner in which he marched through the lands of the Seneca, Onondaga and Cayuga.

Victory in the war brought the Americans their independence from Britain. The Treaty of Paris, signed in 1783, revealed the powerlessness of the Indians to withstand the pressure of White settlement, and the willingness of their European allies to make peace at their expense. The British at first urged that an Indian buffer state be established. In due course, however, British negotiators surrendered all claims to the lands south of the Great Lakes that they, the Canadians or the Indians had held. This betrayal prompted one Iroquois chieftain to reprimand a British official:

> The King surely would not pretend to give the Americans that which was not his to give; and would not believe that the Americans would accept that which the King had not power to give. They were allies of the King, not subjects; and would not submit to such treatment. . . . If England had done so it was an act of cruelty and injustice and capable only of Christians.

All that Britain would agree to do was to resettle her Indian allies north of the Great Lakes. Thus began the movement of the Iroquois into Canada. Many Iroquois, led by Joseph Brant, settled a large tract along both sides of the Grand River in the vicinity of present-day Brantford, Ontario, and others established themselves on the Bay of Quinte.

The condition of the Iroquois was lamentable. The Iroquois Confederacy was a shambles. The Iroquois who remained in the United States had to cede their western lands, and in the confused times that followed New York state officials and land companies negotiated treaties with the separate nations, fragmenting the Iroquois homeland in the United States into small reserves.

But the usefulness of the Iroquois in a military way was not yet ended, at least as far as the British were concerned. In 1812, war broke out between Great Britain and the United States. Britain sought alliances with the Indians. Once again, the Iroquois and other Indians chose to fight on the side of the British, but they fought in pursuit of their own interests. Tecumseh, leader of the Shawnee, believed that an Indian buffer state could be created in the Ohio Valley and that the stream of White settlers crossing the mountains could be checked. The Iroquois were especially effective in the defeat of the Americans at Queenston Heights and at Beaver Dam. To the Indians, including the Iroquois, the War of 1812 was merely a continuation of earlier hostilities, another attempt to defend their homeland.

In the negotiations that led to the Treaty of Ghent, formally bringing the War of 1812 to an end, the British tried to secure an Indian buffer state, but the Americans would not hear of it. Even in their Canadian refuge, after the War of 1812, the Iroquois were soon vastly outnumbered by the White population, reduced to demographic insignificance.

The War of 1812 marked the end of an epoch in which the Indian nations were a military force in the never-ending wars of the Europeans in North America. Diplomacy and alliances had served the Iroquois extremely well for almost two hundred years, but they could not resist the inexorable advance of the agricultural frontier. On the great plains the Indians were still the lords of the soil, still a military force. But out there they would not be seen as potential allies: rather they would be sought and destroyed by the now far superior military power of the United States.

In Canada there was no predisposition to eliminate the indigenous population except through assimilation, to remake the Indians into white people with brown skins. There would be no wars to exterminate the Indians. The White population regarded the Indian culture and way of life as primitive and anomalous. Insofar as they thought about it at all, Canadians were inclined to believe that the Indians had to be taught the arts of civilization and the duties of citizenship. As the Indians moved from what J. R. Miller calls "alliance to irrelevance," the British and their Canadian successors responded with a change of attitude from respect and gratitude to pity and contempt.

When the Spaniards came to the New World, they felt free to massacre the Indians, the Portuguese to enslave them. The Indians were barbarians, their culture deficient, their customs abominable; they could be treated with cruelty and indifference. The destruction of millions was the outcome.

It may be argued that the French and the British were not guilty of slaughter on as great a scale. Indian populations in North America, however, were much smaller than in Central America and South America. The French and the British needed the Indians as partners in the fur trade, and as military allies, but as more and more colonists arrived they needed land. So they sought to make the Indians give up their land, their ideas of land tenure and their claims to distinct political institutions. Unless the Indians assimilated, they could not progress. As a people apart they were despised.

Canadians often think of their country as the peaceable kingdom. But fear and hatred of Indians is sometimes not far beneath the surface. In 1990, when the Mohawks at Kahnawake took down the barricades obstructing access to Montreal, Indian women and children returning to the reserve were pelted with rocks by the angry residents of Chateauguay, while the Quebec Provincial Police stood idly by, refusing to enforce the law or to keep public order.

Today, the Iroquois have been reduced to a few reserves and reservations along the Canada-U.S. border. The establishment, in both Canada and the United States, of elected councils for the Iroquois communities set up tensions between the Iroquois who held to the paramountcy of traditional institutions and those prepared to see changes that many of them thought more suited to the present condition of the communities, tensions that even today divide Iroquois communities in both countries. The tradition of Iroquois sovereignty is used now to justify the transport of cigarettes across the international boundary, establishing casinos free of state control and, at Oka, throwing up armed blockades. This is said by some to be the sole remnant of the authority and tradition of the Six Nations.

But the Iroquois are aware of their remarkable past. They know their Confederacy was once the linchpin of political and military relationships between the European powers in North America. They know that in part at least their Confederacy inspired the framers of the U.S. Constitution. Why should they now accept our view that their institutions, which exhibited such sophistication and adaptability in the past, have lost their efficacy in the present? They hold tenaciously to their belief in the sovereignty of the Six Nations. They still believe in the viability of the Confederacy. They believe in these things not because of an obsession with the past, but because they believe they can be the means to re-establish control over their own lives.

CHAPTER 6

John Marshall and the Indians

In 1963 when I opened my own law practice in Vancouver, I had few clients. Among the few were two Indians from Nanaimo, Clifford White and David Bob, charged with hunting deer in the closed season. At their request I travelled to Nanaimo to talk with Indian elders. The elders spoke of a treaty made in 1854 guaranteeing their hunting rights; they also spoke of Indian title to the land, of aboriginal rights, of Indian sovereignty.

When I had gone to law school in the 1950s, the idea of aboriginal rights had never been discussed. Law schools paid no attention to the issues of Indian land or Indian rights. It was not even a marginal subject, the flame kept burning by a few. No one studied it, and no one thought about it. We all knew in a vague sort of way that the country used to belong to the Indians, but we were not at all curious about how the Indians had governed themselves, about how they treated the question of title to land or even about whether we had any right to take possession of it.

So to prepare for my case I went to the Law Library to read up on the subject. There I came across the judgements of Chief Justice John Marshall, the greatest judge of the new nation forged in the War of Independence. He had written of the things the elders had talked about, of Indian title and Indian sovereignty. Clifford White and David Bob's case went all the way to the Supreme Court of Canada. Along the way we argued not only that they had a treaty but also that if they did not, well, they could rely on their aboriginal right to hunt. We won the case on the ground that the Indians at Nanaimo had entered into a treaty in 1854 recognizing their hunting rights during the closed season. At the same time we raised again the issues discussed in John Marshall's great judgements. In them he articulated in majestic language the concepts of which the Iroquois and other Native peoples across the Americas speak today: Indian title to ancestral lands and Indian sovereignty.

John Marshall was a Virginian, a contemporary of Thomas Jefferson, but, unlike Jefferson, he was not a slaveowner. He was a Federalist, of the party that believed that the new republic had to have a strong federal government. He served as Secretary of State under President John Adams, and then as Chief Justice of the United States, an office he held from 1801 to 1835. He is best known for his landmark judgement in *Marbury v. Madison,* in which the Supreme Court asserted its power of judicial review, and for a series of judgements affirming the powers of the federal government and the rights of private property. But the most profound of all the judgements that he wrote are those dealing with Indian sovereignty and aboriginal title. In these judgements he took up where the debate at Valladolid had left it the moral and intellectual argument regarding the place of the Indians in the political and legal order established in the New World.

The Spanish and the Portuguese struggled with the question of justification for the acquisition of their possessions in the New World. The French and the British, too, sought to justify what they had done, though not with the same conviction as the Iberians. Almost any reason would do. Sometimes it was progress, sometimes Christianity, sometimes the perceived inferiority of Indian culture, sometimes a just war, most often it was the fact of occupation by European settlers on the ground—always there was a reason. But always, at the end of the day, even for the English and the French, there was that one persistent question: how does one people, one race, justify the taking of the lands of another people, another race?

By Marshall's time, the question of justification seemed less important; the takeover of the Atlantic seaboard and the lands east of the Mississippi had already occurred. Instead, the question was, what is to be done in the future? Whatever was to be done had to take account of the past. What was to be the rationale?

John Marshall's judgements represent the most compelling attempt, in the post-colonial era, to work out the implications of the occupation by the United States of Indian land. The United States' experience is important, not only because that country is the greatest nation-state to emerge in the New World, seen as the exemplar of democracy and the rule of law, but also because in the United States Supreme Court's formal rationale for European domination in the New World lies the basis for a fair accommodation of the claims of Native people, not only in the United States but also in other countries.

As settlement took place along the eastern seaboard, and when settlers crossed the Appalachians, and then the Mississippi, the Indians were dispossessed. At intervals, as the Indians were forced back, provision was made by the United States government to make a secure place for them in the lands that still remained to them, in land that was called Indian Country. There was a legal barrier of sorts, but always the barrier separating the frontiersmen from Indian Country came down—indeed, even before it came down it was likely to have been breached in many places—and the Indians had to retreat again. The United States was no more able to restrain its citizens than the king of Spain had been able to check the excesses of the conquistadores, or the British to enforce obedience to the Proclamation Line of 1763.

After the War of Independence the newly constituted United States of America had to develop its own Indian policy. It was a question of determining the relationship the original inhabitants of the continent—still occupying most of it—were to have with the new republic. This was to preoccupy the rulers of the United States well into the late nineteenth century.

The Indians were conceived of as a people apart, a distinct people found everywhere throughout the continent. They were not, however, citizens of the United States; they were not part of the American adventure. But since they occupied land within the United States and virtually all land to the west, they could not be ignored: the White population was migrating westward. So how could the Indians fit into the American federal scheme?

For a time it was thought that a political solution might be possible. After the War of Independence, the British had tried to establish an independent Indian buffer state, but the United States rejected the idea. The United States did, however, consider whether the solution might be geographical—not an independent Indian nation-state, but one of the United States made up exclusively of Indians. The Delawares were the first Indian nation to conclude a treaty with the United States, at Fort Pitt in 1778. Under the treaty, the "territorial rights" of the Delawares were guaranteed, and they were invited, together with other tribes, "to join the present confederation, and to form a state, whereof the Delaware nation shall be the head, and have a representation in Congress." When the Louisiana Purchase was made in 1803, many Americans envisaged that it would contain a consolidated Indian state or states, in every way a part of the Union.

In fact, the idea of an Indian state within the Union persisted for a century. As late as 1871, President Ulysses S. Grant recommended establishing an area south of Kansas for "collecting most of the Indians now between the Missouri and the Pacific and south of the British possessions into one Territory or one State." An Indian state was a means of avoiding the hard questions that would face the United States if the Indians were to live among the Americans, if Indian people and Indian communities were to be found in every state.

At first the United States simply adopted Britain's policy. On 22 September 1783, after the signing of the Treaty of Paris, Congress issued a proclamation affirming United States dominion over all the territory west of the Thirteen Colonies hitherto claimed by Great Britain, and providing that no White person might settle in or purchase lands claimed by Indian peoples "without the express authority" of Congress.

In 1787 Congress passed the Northwest Ordinance, dealing with settlement north of the Ohio River. It enunciated a liberal policy towards the Indians:

> The utmost good faith shall always be observed towards the Indians, their lands and property shall never be taken from them without their consent; and in their property, rights and liberty, they never shall be invaded or disturbed, unless in just and lawful wars authorized by Congress. . . .

But Congress found it convenient, as a matter of practice, to abjure good faith if it entailed the restoration of land to the Indians. To General St. Clair, the Governor of the Northwest Territory, Congress sent special instructions to examine the "treaties which have been made," and told him that, in negotiations with the Indians, the treaties "must not be departed from, unless a change of boundary, beneficial to the United States can be obtained."

All of this occurred during the period of the Articles of Confederation. In 1787, the very year that Congress passed the Northwest Ordinance, the Founding Fathers met at Philadelphia to write a new Constitution. In the Constitution they lodged with Congress exclusive power to make treaties with the Indians.

In 1790, Congress itself, at its first session, passed the Indian Non-Intercourse Act. The Act provided—and still provides—that no one may negotiate or enter into agreements with the Indians without first obtaining federal consent to do so. This was a reiteration of British policy, derived from the Royal Proclamation of 1763.

But these measures hardly impeded at all the westward movement by settlers and their occupation of Indian land. It was impossible for the authorities in Spain, across the Atlantic, to enforce fair dealing between Spaniards and the Indians in the New World. Neither could the United States, two centuries later, enforce fair dealing in its own back yard. The settlers simply ignored the Northwest Ordinance and the Non-Intercourse Act, and the United States could not or would not enforce them.

In the early years of the Republic, one of the main theatres of conflict with the Indians was the old Northwest. Frontiersmen were passing across the Ohio, encroaching on Indian lands. But it was in the south that the clashes between the settlers and the Indians were fiercest. The settlers and the states, especially Georgia, were launching attacks upon the Indians to force them from their lands. In Georgia the Creeks were the leaders of the Indian resistance. President Washington sought a settlement through negotiations with the Creeks. Yet Georgia was unalterably opposed to any settlement short of complete dispossession of the Indians and termination of all their rights.

Washington invited Alexander McGillivray, leader of the Creeks, son of a Scottish father and an Indian mother, to come to New York to meet with him. McGillivray, and some thirty other Indian leaders, travelled north to Federal Hall in New York, then the seat of the United States government. On 7 August 1790, a treaty with the Creeks was signed by President Washington, Secretary of State Jefferson and Secretary of War Knox, and by McGillivray and twenty-three other Creek leaders, with the Chief Justice of New York State and the Mayor of New York City signing as witnesses.

The Creeks ceded a great deal of land in eastern Georgia but they received from the United States a guarantee "in perpetuity" to their remaining lands, including ten million hectares which Georgia had "sold" to three land companies. Moreover, the treaty provided that any citizen of the United States who settled on the lands of the Creek people without permission of the Creeks forfeited the protection of the United States; and that, in any case, entry into the territory of the Creeks was to be made only with the display of a valid Creek passport. The Creeks' right to self-government was acknowledged, and guarantees for their land were provided. Thus were the Creeks' objectives—land and sovereignty—fulfilled.

Georgia objected; James Jackson, representing Georgia in Congress, denounced the affront to his state. Jackson said it was intolerable that President Washington had "invited a savage of the Creek Nation to the seat of government, caressed him in a most extraordinary manner, and sent him loaded with favors." Georgia simply refused to abide by the terms of the treaty that President Washington had signed, and Washington did nothing about it. A pattern had emerged: encroachment by White settlers on Indian lands, failed attempts by the federal government to impose order, further concessions by the Indians, guarantees for the Indians, and then the repetition of the whole process.

The hostility of the State of Georgia towards the Indian tribes, though it coincided with the assertion of states' rights, demonstrates nevertheless the hostility of the states—persisting from the founding of the Republic to the present—towards Native sovereignty and Native land tenure.

President Washington was troubled by his government's inability to protect the Indians. Washington despaired of "anything short of a Chinese wall, or a line of troops" being able to keep land speculators and squatters out of Indian country. Henry Knox, Washington's Secretary of War, wrote of the seizure by frontiersmen and settlers of Indian lands "by force or fraud." He went on:

> As we are more powerful, and more enlightened than they are, there is a responsibility of national character, that we should treat them with kindness, and even liberality. It is a melancholy reflection, that our modes of population have been more destructive to the Indian natives than the conduct of the conquerors of Mexico and Peru. The evidence of this is the utter extirpation of nearly all the Indians in most populous parts of the Union. A future historian may mark the causes of this destruction of the human race in sable colors.

Virtually every president who came after Washington sought—or pretended to seek—federal authority to protect the rights of the Indians, yet each of them surrendered to the settlers' rampant desire for Indian land.

The main theme of United States policy may be observed in Thomas Jefferson's state papers. Jefferson's policy was one of liberal measures to facilitate the assimilation of the Indians. Yet beneath it all, he comprehended that this was something neither Natives nor Whites wanted. Few settlers were prepared to countenance the assimilation of Indians if that meant Indians could keep their land. In Georgia, the Cherokees, for example, like the Creeks, had given up Indian ways and adopted White institutions. Assimilation was, however, not enough. When settlers wanted their land, the Cherokees, assimilated or not, were removed from it.

The idea of a general removal of the eastern Indians to the Great Plains beyond the Mississippi, a region thought to be uninhabitable, was mooted by Jefferson (whose acquisition of Louisiana in 1803 made it possible), favoured by James Madison, adopted by James Monroe and energetically pursued under Andrew Jackson and Martin Van Buren. Thus emerged the policy of removal: the acquisition of Indian lands for the settlers, and the expulsion of the Indians from their ancestral places. An Indian Country was created west of a boundary (much like the earlier Proclamation line) running from Canada to Texas.

In this way, the Americans occupied more and more of the continent. But the great issue put to the Spaniards by Las Casas had not been addressed; at any rate, no formal answer had been made: What right did the Americans have to dispossess the Indians? The Americans had to consider two questions: What was the foundation in law for American sovereignty? Where did the Indians fit in?

It was John Marshall who, in a series of judgements written in the 1820s and 1830s, undertook to describe the relationship between American sovereignty and Indian self-government and between American dominion over the land and Indian title. Marshall took the policy of the British, as laid down in the Royal Proclamation of 1763, as his starting point. He accepted the legitimacy of Native sovereignty, Native institutions and Native title to the land and wove them into the American system.

When the Europeans discovered, then began to colonize North America, the Indians regarded themselves as the rightful owners of the land. They were the original occupants of the land, and each tribe traditionally held its own tribal territory, a territory that other tribes also recognized. By what theory, asked Marshall, did Europeans rule over the continent that was 'new' only in their eyes? By what title did they acquire sovereignty over these new lands?

The European nations waged wars among themselves when one nation sought to wrest newly discovered territory from another, and the results of these wars always left one European nation or another claiming sovereignty over the territory in dispute. It did not occur to the Europeans that the Indians might retain sovereignty over the lands. Nevertheless, according to Marshall, the European powers did acknowledge that the Indians, as the original occupants, retained an interest—a legal interest—in their lands. This legal interest came to be known as aboriginal title, or Indian title.

In 1776, the signatories to the Declaration of Independence had declared their belief in the Laws of Nature and of Nature's God. Natural law was a powerful influence in U.S. constitutionalism and in the formation of United States jurisprudence. Every man had inherent rights, not simply those rights that the state acknowledged.

What about Black slaves? Did they not have a natural right to liberty? Not really. Blacks were thought to be inferior; in any event they were aliens, entering the country as slaves, the property of their masters. In those days property was deemed essential to liberty. Property made a man independent both economically and politically. If you took away a man's property, you took away his liberty. So the case of Black slaves was singular; if you took away a man's slaves, you impaired his liberty.

With the Indians, the rejection of natural law was more complicated. "Next to the black race within our bosom," James Madison, the man who was the principal author of the United States Constitution, wrote in 1824, "that of the red on our borders is the policy most baffling to the country." Indeed, perhaps, more baffling.

Unlike Black slaves, Indians were not perceived to be linked to the future economic development of the nation, an attitude which persists today. They were seen as obstacles to civilization, progress and westward expansion; if incapable of being civilized, they must be removed. But the justification for denying Indians the rights flowing from natural law was more difficult than it was in the case of Black slaves. The Indians were claiming rights as the original inhabitants; the land was their property; and they were free men, not themselves property. Their nations had been recognized as sovereign; treaties had been made with them.

But set against these propositions was another set of propositions: the Indians' failure to conform to civilized norms, their warlike character and their failure to treat land as a source of income. Furthermore, they were said to be incorrigible, they would not or could not change. Therefore the Indians' natural right to autonomy and to retain their land had to be rejected. The United States would not consider that another culture and way of life, so different from that of the dominant society, could be permitted to hold sway except in isolated pockets of the country.

John Marshall sought to reconcile Europe's triumph with the idea of the rule of law. He wrote about the precepts of international law and how they should be applied to the Europeans' acquisition of America. Marshall did not rely on Europe's Christianizing or civilizing mission. Instead he enunciated the principle of discovery: the Europeans had discovered America, and this gave them sovereignty over the indigenous people of America and dominion over the land. This brought Marshall to the important practical questions. Essentially, he said, Europeans had taken the land. But this did not mean the Indian tribes had no rights thereafter. In 1823, in a case called *Johnson v. McIntosh,* he said:

> In the establishment of . . . relations . . . [between Europeans and Indians] the rights of the original inhabitants were, in no instance, entirely disregarded; but were necessarily, to a considerable extent, impaired. They were admitted to be the rightful occupants of the soil, with a legal as well as just claim to retain possession of it, and to use it according to their own discretion; but their rights to complete sovereignty, as independent nations, were necessarily diminished and their power to dispose of the soil at their own will, to whomsoever they pleased, was denied by the original fundamental principle that discovery gave exclusive title to those who made it.

By this reasoning Marshall held that the natural right to dispose of their property did not apply to Indians. The Indians had no power to sell their land, except to the federal government. This was a fundamental principle, derived from the Royal Proclamation of 1763, and designed to protect the Indians. Only the federal government could buy Indian lands; only the federal government could convey title to Indian lands. The courts of the United States would enforce a purchaser's claim to Indian land only if he had bought it from the government of the United States.

Land and sovereignty were seen, then as now, to be the two vital elements in the consideration of the rights of the Indians. The assumption of sovereignty by the United States did not extinguish Indian title nor deny tribal sovereignty; these were, however, as Marshall wrote, "necessarily diminished." The whole edifice was founded on the theory of discovery; no one who thought about it, however, was altogether satisfied with this.

In 1828, in an address, Marshall's colleague Justice Joseph Story asked why the Indians, as possessors of the land, could not "maintain their right to share in the common inheritance" by "stand[ing] upon the eternal laws of natural justice." Story answered that natural law "was quite too refined to satisfy the ambition and lust for dominion" of the early European settlers. They therefore created the convenient doctrine that "the Natives possessed a present right of occupancy which might be surrendered to the discovering nation." The issue was "whether the country itself shall be abandoned by civilized man, or maintained by his sword as the right of the strongest."

Marshall's theories did not sit well with the states. In 1828, the Georgia state assembly annexed the lands of the Cherokees, established state courts and police on Cherokee land, annulled all tribal laws and imprisoned tribal officials. When a Cherokee, George Corn Tassels, was indicted for murder of another Cherokee, the state superior court held that the Georgia courts, not the Cherokee tribal courts, had jurisdiction, on the ground that savages could have no lawful government. It followed the reasoning of philosopher Thomas Hobbes, who had written that such a people, "having no government at all," had no right to remain in possession of their land.

As well as having no government, the Indians' use of the lands they held was considered deficient. In 1830 Madison, in a letter to William Wirt, counsel for the Cherokees, argued that: "[By] not incorporating their labour and associating fixed improvements with the soil, they have not appropriated it to themselves, nor made the destined use of its capacity for increasing the number and enjoyments of the human race."

The Cherokees, however, did not fall neatly into Madison's thesis. Many of them had given up hunting, had become farmers, established schools and adopted White institutions. In fact, Georgia wanted to remove the Cherokees, assimilated or not, altogether from their lands. President Andrew Jackson had brought in a removal bill in 1829. Madison thought this would be for the best. As he wrote to Wirt: "It is so evident that they can never be tranquil or happy, within the bounds of a State, either in a separate or subject character. Removal to another home, if a good one can be found, may well be the wish of their best friends."

Wirt, replying to Madison, disposed of the theory of discovery and of the proposition that the Cherokees should be removed from their lands:

> The argument against the title of the Indians to their land, compared with the argument in favour of our title to them, presents the strangest absurdity. . . . We say . . . that they can have no title but to so much land as they can now cultivate; . . . whilst we hold that we have a perfect title to millions upon millions of acres confessedly beyond our present capacity for cultivation. In [the Cherokees'] improved condition as civilized agriculturalists, you will perceive that the argument drawn from writers on natural law, applied to them in their savage state, is unanswerable, unless we admit the new and strange ground, now taken, that they had no right to alter their condition and become husbandmen.

An appeal was taken in Tassels's case to the Supreme Court of the United States. Georgia had Tassels executed at once, making the case moot. The Cherokee nation then sought from the Supreme Court a general injunction against Georgia. The case is called *Cherokee Nation v. Georgia*. In his judgement in the *Cherokee Nation* case John Marshall wrote:

> If courts were permitted to indulge their sympathies, a case better calculated to excite them can scarcely be imagined. A people once numerous, powerful, and truly independent, found by our ancestors in the quiet and uncontrolled possession of an ample domain, gradually sinking beneath our superior policy, our arts and our arms, have yielded their lands by successive treaties, each of which contains a solemn guarantee of the residue, until they retain no more of their formerly extensive territory than is deemed necessary to their comfortable subsistence.

But Marshall held against the Cherokees. Under Article III of the Constitution of the United States the Supreme Court could only hear "Controversies between two or more states; between a state and citizens of another state; between citizens of different states; and between a state or the citizens thereof and foreign states, citizens or subjects." The Cherokee Nation was not a State of the Union. Was it then a "foreign state"? Marshall said no. So, the Court declined to hear the case. But if the Cherokee nation was not a foreign state, what was it?

Marshall felt obliged to address this question, and in so doing developed his theory of Indian tribes as "domestic, dependent nations":

> Though the Indians are acknowledged to have an unquestionable, and therefore, unquestioned right to the lands they occupy, until that right shall be extinguished by a voluntary cession to our government; yet it may well be doubted whether those tribes which reside within the acknowledged boundaries of the United States can, with strict accuracy, be denominated foreign nations. They may, more correctly, perhaps be denominated domestic dependent nations. They occupy a territory to which we assert title independent of their will, which must take effect in point of possession when their right of possession ceases. Meanwhile they are in a state of pupillage. Their relation to the United States resembles that of a ward to his guardian.

Justice William Johnson, in the same case, in a concurring opinion, expressed Georgia's uncluttered view of Indians, describing them as "nothing more than wandering hordes, held together only by ties of blood and habit, and having neither laws or government, beyond what is required in a savage state."

The Cherokees, not satisfied with this dismissal of their case on technical grounds, came back the next term with a case that the Court was bound to hear on its merits. Samuel Worcester, a New England missionary, had been imprisoned by Georgia for entering Cherokee territory without a pass from the state government. In this famous case, called *Worcester v. Georgia,* Marshall returned to the question, by what right did the United States take Indian lands? The idea of natural law was not dead. Justice John McLean, in a concurring judgement, refuted what Justice Johnson had said in *Cherokee Nation v. Georgia.* He declared that the "abstract right of every sector of the human race to a reasonable portion of the soil, by which to acquire the means of subsistence, cannot be controverted." The "law of nature" he said, "is paramount to all other laws."

Marshall himself, in a passage that has been cited throughout the English-speaking world, began by wondering aloud about his own theory of discovery.

> It is difficult to comprehend the proposition that the inhabitants of either quarter of the globe could have rightful original claims of dominion over the inhabitants of the other, or over the lands they occupied; or that the discovery of either by the other should give the discoverer rights in the country discovered which annulled the pre-existing rights of its ancient possessors.

The Europeans found America, he said,

> . . . in possession of a people who had made small progress in agriculture or manufactures, and whose general employment was war, hunting and fishing. Did these adventurers, by sailing along the coast and occasionally landing on it, acquire for the several governments to whom they belonged, or by whom they were commissioned, a rightful property in the soil from the Atlantic to the Pacific; or rightful dominion over the numerous people who occupied it? Or has nature, or the great Creator of all things, conferred these rights over hunters and fishermen, on agriculturalists and manufacturers?

Marshall was skeptical, but the practical world beckoned. He answered the question in these words:

> But power, war, conquest, give rights, which after possession, are conceded by the world; and which can never be controverted by those on whom they descend. We proceed, then, to the actual state of things, having glanced at their origin, because holding it in our recollection might shed some light on existing pretensions.

He went on to discuss the principle of discovery:

This principle, acknowledged by all Europeans, because it was the interest of all to acknowledge it, gave to the nation making the discovery, as its inevitable consequence, the sole right of acquiring the soil and of making settlements upon it. It was an exclusive principle which shut out the right of competition among those who had agreed to it; not one which could annul the previous rights of those who had not agreed to it. It regulated the right given by discovery among the European discoverers, but could not affect the rights of those already in possession, either as aboriginal occupants, or as occupants by virtue of a discovery made before the memory of man.

Discovery, though it justified the acquisition of the lands claimed by the Europeans, did not extinguish, though it necessarily diminished, the rights of the Indians. Marshall, writing for a unanimous court (Justice Johnson had in the meantime retired), held that Georgia's laws were "repugnant to the Constitution, laws and treaties of the United States." He held that Georgia state laws did not apply on the Cherokee Reservation. He went on:

The Indian nations had always been considered as distinct, independent political communities, retaining their original rights, as the undisputed possessors of the soil, from time immemorial, with the single exception of that imposed by irresistible power, which excluded them from intercourse with any other European potentate than the first discoverer of the coast of the particular region claimed. . . . The very term "nation" so generally applied to them, means "a people distinct from others."
    . . . The words "treaty" and "nation" are words of our own language, selected in our diplomatic and legislative proceedings, by ourselves, having each a definite and well understood meaning. We have applied them to Indians, as we have applied them to the other nations of the earth. They are applied to all in the same sense. . . .

The Constitution, Marshall explained, "by declaring treaties already made, as well as those to be made, to be the supreme law of the land, has adopted and sanctioned the previous treaties with the Indian nations, and consequently admits their rank among those powers who are capable of making treaties." The treaty relationship, he said "was that of a nation claiming and receiving the protection of one more powerful, not that of individuals abandoning their national character, and submitting as subjects to the laws of a master." The tribes were no different, he said, than many small nations of Europe: "A weak state in order to provide for its safety, may place itself under the protection of one more powerful without stripping itself of the right of government, and ceasing to be a State." He continued: "The Cherokee nation, then, is a distinct community, occupying its own territory, with boundaries accurately described, in which the laws of Georgia can have no force. . . . The whole intercourse between the United States and this nation, is, by our constitution and laws, vested in the government of the United States."

So the Indians were to be considered as *nations,* with rights to the land that could not be denied, peoples entitled to a measure of self-government.

Marshall's powerful judgements were acts of judicial statecraft. They put in place a theory of Indian sovereignty and aboriginal title. Leaving moral obligations and high-minded concepts of abstract justice to one side, the law of the United States acknowledges that the Indians have a legal interest in their ancestral lands and sovereignty that is unextinguished, though restricted in its scope.

This was all very fine. But Americans believed that they had a duty to develop the earth's resources, a duty that justified them in dispossessing the Indians. Land should be worked for the profit it could yield; an owner who did not profit from the land did not deserve to hold it.

President Jackson rejected the Supreme Court's decision in *Worcester v. Georgia.* Jackson believed that the Indians could no longer exist as independent enclaves within the states. Indians, if they did not become subject to state law, must be removed. This same inability to see Indian governments as an integral part of the constitutional arrangements of the United States, not "foreign" but indigenous, persists to this day.

Jackson allowed the state of Georgia to assume jurisdiction over Cherokee lands by refusing to enforce Marshall's decision in *Worcester v. Georgia.* He is supposed to have said, "John Marshall has made his judgement, now let him enforce it!" He concluded that the "solution" to the Indian problem was to set apart an area west of the Mississippi, to be guaranteed to the Indian tribes as long as they occupied it.

Was there any link between the plight of native Americans and the condition of the Black population? Not really. The Blacks were concentrated in the South, and were required to remain on the land as labourers in the fields. The Indians, on the other hand, were forced to leave the land. Even when freed, Blacks remained a part of the life of the urban industrial America beginning to emerge in the North. Notwithstanding schemes such as those espoused by Lincoln and Grant for Black emigration to Africa or the West Indies, Blacks regarded themselves as part of America—indeed, their struggle has been to integrate, to achieve "equal protection."

Nor was the situation of ethnic minorities comparable to that of the Indians. Seen from a Native point of view, these minorities are merely a part of the advancing European monolith. Of course, ethnic minorities have sometimes been excluded from the advantages of membership in the dominant society, but their goal has always been to participate in the dominant society, not to be a people apart.

The Indians *did,* however, desire to remain a people apart, a distinct people within America, governing themselves on their own lands. The law was on their side. John Marshall's judgements were—and still are—the law of the United States. Congress has, from time to time, sought to diminish Indian sovereignty, and Marshall's successors on the Supreme Court, from time to time, have limited the scope of Marshall's judgements. Indeed, many of their judgements illustrate how easily the law may be overthrown by judges when their deepest biases are implicated. If they deny the legitimacy of Native history and Native culture, where does that leave Native rights?

In 1955, in the *Tee-Hit Ton* case, the Supreme Court of the United States had before it a claim by the Tlingit Indians of the Alaska Panhandle. In Alaska, unlike in the contiguous forty-eight states, Native people, Indians, Eskimos and Aleuts, did not sign any treaty. There was no surrender of what is now Alaska by the Native peoples. In the *Tee-Hit Ton* case, the Indians claimed that their lands had been taken without compensation. They had Indian title—everyone acknowledged it; there had been no treaty, no surrender of their lands. The Indians claimed that, like other Americans, their title to land could not be taken without compensation. The Fifth Amendment of the

United States Constitution provides that no one's property may be taken without compensation. But the Supreme Court held that the Fifth Amendment did not apply to Indian lands held under aboriginal title; such lands were regarded as vacant lands at the disposal of the federal government. The Court held that Congress had plenary or absolute power over Indian land. Indian title was an interesting phrase, but not a great deal more. The law was for White people, not for Indians.

Such attitudes are more important than constitutions and laws. If the judges in the *Tee-Hit Ton* case had perceived Native society and values as authentic, they would have had no difficulty in extending Fifth Amendment protection to Indian land held under aboriginal title. Why should farmers living off the land, but not Indians living off the land, be entitled to Fifth Amendment protection? The legal arguments are pure sophistry. The judges believed that one form of use and occupation is valid and the other is not; one way of life is valid, the other is not.

This is our view today. We believe in a linear idea of progress, the movement of humankind through stages: first hunting and gathering, then agriculture, finally urban, industrial civilization. Europe represents an advanced stage of development, the Indians a primitive stage.

Nevertheless, John Marshall's reasoning was so powerfully stated, his judgements so compelling, that they guide courts all over the world even today. Lawyers and judges anxious to locate a lawful foundation for relations between Whites and Natives invariably turn to them. The courts of the United States are still guided by Marshall's words. So are the Canadian courts. In 1990, in *R. v. Sparrow,* a fishing rights case arising in British Columbia, the Supreme Court of Canada expressly adopted Marshall's views in *Johnson v. McIntosh.* But the jurisprudence of both countries is still at variance with the attitudes of many legislators. As President Jackson demonstrated, the expression of legal principles is not enough. Events on the ground, the innate prejudices of men, not laws, no matter how carefully crafted, are the determinants of Indian rights.

Even Jackson was prepared, however, once the tribes had been removed from lands sought for White settlement, to acquiesce in their right to live autonomously in the lands still held by them. Jackson acknowledged the idea of Indian Country, but it would simply be farther to the west, beyond existing White settlements, where Indians would live free from White control. The *Indian Non-Intercourse Act* of 1834 provided a statutory definition of Indian Country:

> [A]ll that part of the United States west of the Mississippi, and not within the states of Missouri and Louisiana, or the territory of Arkansas, and, also, that part of the United States east of the Mississippi, and not within any state to which the Indian title has not been extinguished, for the purposes of this Act, [shall be] deemed to be the Indian country,

This definition remained on the statute books of the United States until the general statutory revision of 1874 when it was deleted, westward expansion having made it obsolete. Indian Country continued to shrink.

By 1840, nearly all the Indians east of the Mississippi had been removed west of that great river. But now the settlers were headed for Indian Country; they, too, were about to cross the Mississippi, to occupy the great plains, which only a few years before had been thought to be uninhabitable by Europeans.

John Marshall, like Las Casas before him, had insisted upon the survival of Indian land rights and Indian self-government under the new European dispensation. Marshall was prepared to acknowledge that the tribes were nations, to recognize their tribal governments as political institutions exercising limited sovereignty, over ancestral lands to which they had aboriginal title.

John Marshall's judgements form the basis of our thinking on land claims and Indian self government today. His writings, surveying history, politics and law, have had a unique impact. His analysis has been the basis for asserting the claims of Native people not only in the United States but also in Canada and in most of the countries throughout the world where indigenous peoples claim rights under legal regimes derived from English common law. They are the blueprint for the acknowledgement of Indian land claims and Indian sovereignty in our own time.

CHAPTER 7

Wars Against the Indians:
The United States and Argentina

As John Marshall was writing, Indians were being uprooted and removed beyond the Mississippi. President Andrew Jackson had introduced his removal bill in 1829; it was passed in May 1830. In the decade following, almost 100,000 Indians east of the Mississippi were removed westward, leaving their homelands in the eastern United States open to settlement.

Most tribes signed removal treaties, but there were a few exceptions. The Iroquois who were left in New York insisted on remaining there, and because no one was seeking their lands, they made good their refusal. All of the removals were tragic, but especially the treatment of the so-called Five Civilized Tribes in the South: the Cherokees, Creeks, Choctaws, Chickasaws and Seminoles. After Andrew Jackson declined to enforce John Marshall's ruling affirming the

Cherokees' right to govern themselves on their own land, the state of Georgia gave their lands over to squatters and speculators. The Cherokees were forced to leave. The Creeks, Choctaws and Chickasaws were treated similarly by Mississippi and Alabama. The removal of these tribes, under escort by the United States Army, is known to Native people as the Trail of Tears, because of the loss of thousands of Indian lives through exhaustion, hunger and sickness on the long journey westward. Only about 1,200 Indians remained in the eastern United States of all the tribes that had once lived there.

Of course there were already Indians living beyond the Mississippi, who considered those territories to be their homeland. Between the Mississippi and the far side of the Rockies they numbered at least 200,000. The United States government regarded the great plains as a desert and was content at first to leave the country in the possession of the Indians. A few Army posts were located along the eastern edge of the plains, and a scattering of fur trading posts was to be found.

The Indians of the plains were themselves relative newcomers. In 1492 the great plains were sparsely inhabited. Indian tribes living on the fringes of the plains were agricultural. All of this changed with the advent of the horse.

Cortés had brought ten stallions and five mares to Mexico. In 1598, when the Spanish crossed the Rio Grande to establish New Mexico, they came with seven thousand horses. The revolt of the Pueblo Indians in 1680 forced the Spanish to flee and abandon their animals. The stock that became wild was tamed by the Indians, and traded from tribe to tribe.

By the end of the eighteenth century the Sioux, Cheyenne, Kiowa, Comanche, Crow and Arapaho, on horseback, had entered the plains in pursuit of the buffalo, which provided most of their material needs—meat, clothing, even skins for their tipis. The new material culture based on the buffalo spread over the grasslands and into the Rockies. The Indians had made the plains their home.

But the Indians were not to remain the undisputed masters of their new homeland. Pioneers had discovered that the grasslands of the prairies were fertile. In 1845 the United States annexed Texas. In 1846 the Oregon Treaty was signed. In the Mexican War of 1846–48, the United States seized the Southwest and California. By

mid-century the time had come for the United States to take possession of the west beyond the Mississippi. This drive to populate and
exploit the great plains led to the United States Indian wars. These
were wars waged by the United States against the Indians, not wars
between Europeans in which the Indians were sought as allies, but
wars intended to evict the plains Indians from their homeland.

The discovery of gold in California in 1849 led to an influx of gold
seekers making their way across the plains, and treaties were made
with the Indians to extinguish their title to land along the overland
routes to the Pacific. Manifest Destiny became a rallying cry for a society bent on exploration and exploitation of the lands, minerals and
other resources of the land beyond the Mississippi. The streams of
wagon trains moving along the trails through Indian Country, the
slaughter by settlers of buffalo and mountain game on which the Indians depended for subsistence, led inevitably to clashes.

The *Homestead Act* of 1862 encouraged widespread settlement of
the west. Railways, penetrating deeply into the heart of Indian country, were instrumental in the occupation of the plains and the
destruction of the buffalo; furthermore they guaranteed rapid movement of White military power wherever needed. By mid-century it
was obvious that the United States would take possession of the
great plains. Yet the Indians could not be removed: if they were
evicted, where would they be sent? Still farther west? No. Settlers
were already streaming into California.

A new policy became essential, and it turned out to be a different
form of removal; the Indians were placed on "reservations." These
reservation lands would be identified and surveyed, and protected
against encroachment by settlers. On the reservations, it was argued,
Indians would still be able to govern themselves. The reservations
would still be Indian Country, though greatly diminished in extent.

To implement this policy treaties were made in the 1850s and
1860s. The Indians could see the Whites advancing everywhere.
Seeking a measure of security, they signed. But their comprehension
of the full significance of the treaties is doubtful. Many Indians had
not signed, or had not authorized those who did sign to do so on
their behalf.

The Indians were not inclined to accept the reservation system, or
to remain there once reservations were established. Even when Indians settled on reservations, they were liable to attack by settlers.

Certainly, the settlers were not disposed to accept reservation boundaries when they wanted land that had been secured to the Indians by treaty.

Even during the Civil War there were clashes between settlers and Indians in the West. The local militias were especially savage. The Colorado volunteers massacred Cheyennes at Sand Creek on 29 November 1864, slaughtering men, women and children asleep in their camp. After hostilities between North and South had ended, the Indian wars resumed with greater intensity. As Robert M. Utley has said, "After Appomattox the nation faced west." For the next twenty-five years the United States made war against the Indians, in a series of campaigns of virtual extermination, that lasted from the close of the Civil War until 1890.

Both General William Tecumseh Sherman, who, after the war, commanded the United States troops on the great plains, and General Philip Sheridan, who served under him, heroes of the Civil War, at one time or another called for the extermination of the Indians. Even General Ulysses S. Grant, a Republican candidate in 1868, echoed the call. Needless to say, it was a cry taken up by many of the frontiersmen. Just as Sherman had undertaken total war against the South, he and his generals conducted total war against the Indians. Grant, once elected, officially adopted a policy of peace, but there was to be no peace for the Indians of the West.

The Indian wars are etched in the American imagination. The tribes of the plains were the first mounted Indian warriors Americans had fought. To be sure, they were vanquished by the United States Army. Nevertheless, they fought courageously in a cause that was doomed. The Indian wars culminated in 1876 and 1877 in two famous encounters between the Army and the Sioux, and between the Army and the Nez Percé.

For Americans, the golden-haired General George Custer is the most evocative symbol of the Indian wars. But the campaigns that the United States Army waged in these Indian wars were not chivalrous or gallant. Indian women and children died along with Indian warriors. The Army's strategy was to destroy the Indians' camps, ponies, food and forage. Custer's Last Stand was an ignominious defeat inflicted on a commander carrying out an odious policy. The events leading to the Little Big Horn are a metaphor for the betrayal of promises that led to the Indian wars.

The Great Sioux Reservation, including the Black Hills of what is now South Dakota, had been set aside by the Fort Laramie Treaty in 1868. But, like other reservations, it had been subject to invasion by frontiersmen. Miners rushed into the Black Hills of the Great Sioux Reservation in search of gold. The Indians, said President Grant, in 1876, in his last State of the Union Address, were not safe from the "avarice of the white man" who had "violated our treaty stipulations in his search for gold." Having condemned those who had invaded lands promised by treaty to the Sioux, Grant posed the obvious question: "Why . . . [has not] the Government enforced obedience to the terms of the treaty?"

The answer, he said, was "simple"; it lay in numbers and greed. The first frontiersmen entering the Black Hills had been evicted by the troops, but then "gold had been found in paying quantity, and the effort to remove the miners would only result in the desertion of the troops that might be sent there to remove them." Grant then matter-of-factly said, "all difficulty in this matter has, however, been removed—subject to the approval of Congress—by a treaty ceding the Black Hills and approaches to settlement. . . . " Quite easily done—a paradigm of U.S. policy. Aboriginal title, solemn treaties and the goodwill of presidents were never enough to protect the Indians. Presidents capitulated to demands for cession of more and more Indian land. First the treaties, then the reservations had to go.

Law was now to be used not to protect the Sioux on their reservation but to evict them from it. The federal government ordered the Indians to move into a reduced reserve by 31 January 1876. Those who did not would be treated as outlaws. The United States Army moved in to evict the Sioux. Custer led the first column; his target was an Indian village in the Rosebud Valley. But along the route of march Chief Crazy Horse ambushed the column, killing Custer and all of his men at the Little Big Horn. In retaliation, the United States cavalry decided to attack. Any Indian target would do, Sioux or not: so the cavalry destroyed a sleeping Cheyenne village in the Powder River. Sitting Bull, Chief of the Cheyennes, escaped to Canada. It was not a heroic moment for the United States Army.

The clash which endures in the American consciousness as Custer's Last Stand was one with the Sioux, a plains tribe. But the last great campaign was waged against a tribe from the northwest, the Nez Percé.

The Nez Percé had occupied the plateau land where Washington, Oregon and Idaho come together. By the end of the eighteenth century, the Nez Percé had become renowned breeders of horses and hunted buffalo on the plains, though they continued to return regularly to their villages in the mountains.

In 1860, White trespassers found gold on Nez Percé land. New towns sprang up, crowding the Indian villages. In 1863, a treaty was signed which reduced the Indians' reservation land to less than one-quarter of its previous size. Two-thirds of the tribal leaders refused to sign the document, among them the Nez Percé of the Wallowa Valley. In 1871 settlers moved into the Wallowa Valley. The leader of the Nez Percé of Wallowa, Chief Joseph, protested, and in 1873 President Grant formally set aside the Wallowa "as a reservation for the roaming Nez Percé Indians" and ordered the White intruders to withdraw.

The settlers refused to move and threatened to exterminate Chief Joseph's people if they did not leave the valley. As ever siding with the settlers, the United States government decided that the Nez Percé must move on. The Bureau of Indian Affairs ordered that, unless Chief Joseph's people voluntarily came onto the reservation in Idaho set aside for them and others by 1 April 1877, they would be taken there by force. It was almost an exact repetition of the order of a year before that had started the hostilities with the Sioux that resulted in the Custer debacle.

When the Nez Percé did not comply with the Bureau's order, the United States Army was dispatched to round them up. A troop of cavalry caught up with them at White Bird Canyon. The Nez Percé routed the cavalry and thirty-four U.S. soldiers were killed. The rest of the troop fled. Only one Indian died.

News of this defeat aroused the nation. Reinforcements were sent. In the meantime the Nez Percé, having crossed the Salmon River, reached the Clearwater River, where, though greatly outnumbered, they held off the United States forces until they could withdraw again. Then the Indians set off across the Bitterroot Mountains, driving some two thousand horses with them. After nine days in the mountains, they reached Bitterroot Valley, and made camp on an open meadow beside the Big Hole River, where the United States forces launched a surprise attack on them, killing men, women and children. Once more the Indian warriors held them off, seizing a U.S. Army howitzer and rolling it over a steep bluff. As well they captured two thousand rounds of ammunition before breaking off the engagement and retreating again, across Montana, intending, like Sitting Bull, to seek refuge in Canada.

After crossing the Continental Divide and entering the Yellowstone, the Nez Percé turned north. They were still able to hold off the troops, but they were weary, cold and hungry. Still another troop of cavalry was hastening across Montana to intercept them. On the morning of 30 September, the cavalry attacked the Nez Percé camp on the northern edge of the Bear Paw Mountains—only fifty kilometres from the Canadian border. The assault caught the Nez Percé by surprise. Some fled to the north; of these many died of hunger and exposure, though a few made their way to Canada. Nez Percé warriors, however, engaged the cavalry, inflicting heavy casualties on the troopers. The Army laid siege to the camp, as the weather grew colder and snow fell.

When reinforcements arrived, strengthening the forces opposed to him, Chief Joseph left the Indian camp and rode to the Army lines, dismounted and handed over his rifle. Then he spoke the words that have become the requiem for the Indians of the plains:

> I am tired of fighting. Our chiefs are killed. Looking Glass is dead. Toohoolhoolzote is dead. The old men are all dead. It is cold and we have no blankets. The little children are freezing to death. My people, some of them, have run away to the hills, and have no blankets, no food; no one knows where they are— perhaps freezing to death. I want to have time to look for my children and see how many I can find. Maybe I shall find them among the dead. Hear me, my chiefs. I am tired; my heart is sick and sad. From where the sun now stands, I will fight no more forever.

With the surrender of Chief Joseph's Nez Percé in 1877 the wars against the American Indian were over but for a few scattered encounters. At Wounded Knee, in 1896, the last cavalry charge annihilated a defenceless Indian village.

The aftermath of Chief Joseph's surrender was as tragic as the defeat of the Nez Percé itself. Chief Joseph had surrendered on the strength of a promise that the Nez Percé would be allowed to return to Idaho, to live there on a reservation. The promise was not kept. The Nez Percé were sent to a reservation in Oklahoma, far from their ancestral lands. Like other Indians of the plains, they have, ever since, mourned their lost freedom.

Almost at the same time, a similar passage of arms was taking place in South America. In Argentina, as in the United States, a population of European descent sought to expand into a hinterland occupied by Indians. In Argentina, however, not even the legal scruples that intermittently preoccupied the United States stood in the way of Argentinian expansion southward to occupy the lands that stretch from the Rio de la Plata to Tierra del Fuego.

Between the Rio de la Plata and the Rio Negro lie the grassy plains called the pampas. South of the Rio Negro are the windswept lands of Patagonia and, beyond, Tierra del Fuego, ringed by mountains. These lands were the homeland of nomadic Indian tribes before any European set foot in what is now Argentina.

The Plata estuary was explored by Sebastian Cabot in the 1520s, who was searching for the kingdom of the Incas. In 1536, Spanish settlers arrived at the mouth of the Rio de la Plata, near the place where Buenos Aires now stands, and established a settlement. In addition to the "fair winds," the site provided a harbour and access along the river to the interior. The Indians of the pampas resisted the establishment of a settlement on land they believed to be theirs; they harried the settlers until they quit the site and returned to Spain.

The fleeing settlers left their horses behind. The abandoned animals moved out onto the grasslands and began to multiply. Within a few generations thousands of them roamed the great hinterland beyond the estuary. The Indians of the pampas captured the horses and soon they became skilled horsemen. Mounted, they were able to hunt down with ease their traditional game, the guanaco, a small mammal about the size of a deer. Moreover, for the Indians mare's meat and mare's blood became one of the mainstays of their diet.

In 1580, when Spanish settlers arrived again at Buenos Aires, the opposition they faced from the Indians was even more fierce than it had been a half-century before. The Indians, on horseback now, drove off the settlers' cattle. Houses were destroyed, horses stolen, families killed. Few Spaniards dared venture beyond the settlement itself. From time to time cavalry expeditions were organized from

Buenos Aires to drive the Indians back. But always the Indians returned. For more than a hundred years, settlers continued to arrive, but the community grew slowly.

At the same time Spaniards were moving south from Peru, along the Pacific coast. When they entered the central plains of Chile they met with steady resistance from the Araucanian Indians, who had earlier fought the Incas, refusing to be absorbed into the Inca empire.

Like the Indians of the pampas, the Araucanians also adopted the horse, which allowed them to launch sudden attacks on the Spaniards and then to retreat into the Andes. In their search for horses, the Araucanians began to make forays across the Andes into the pampas. This led to trade with the Indians of the pampas, a relationship that linked Indians on both sides of the Andes for two hundred years.

What began as simple horse trading soon developed into one of the largest cattle-rustling operations in history. By the early 1700s, the Araucanians had begun to attack the cattle ranches around Buenos Aires, herding the cattle back towards the safety of the mountains. These cattle found their way to Spanish ranchers in Chile, who were willing to pay good prices for cattle that they did not have to import from Europe. Before long, the Indians of the Argentine plains had joined the raiding parties and were an integral part of the trade across the Andes.

The Araucanians came to dominate the peoples of the pampas politically as well as economically. Calfucura, the most famous of the Araucanian chiefs, has been described by an Argentine military historian as "astute and intelligent, a warrior, politically able and an active trader." Like so many other Araucanians, Calfucura made Argentina his home.

By the early 1800s, the Araucanians and the Indians of the pampas had become a single cultural group. Whereas once the Indians of the pampas had travelled in family bands, searching for guanaco, now they were part of a warrior nation, organized in a political and economic network that extended from the Atlantic to the Pacific. They still travelled the plains with their skin tents, but their diet now included beef, along with mare's meat and guanaco. They had adopted a single language—Araucanian. The Iroquois Confederacy preceded the advent of the Europeans, but here on the pampas the Indians had established a confederacy to meet the challenge of the Spanish invasion.

In 1810, seven years after the United States extended its boundaries far to the west by the Louisiana Purchase, Argentina won its independence from Spain. At the time the country consisted of a thin band of settlement, 600 kilometres wide and no more than 200 kilometres from north to south. The rest of what is now Argentina—the hinterland extending 800 kilometres to the north and 2,000 kilometres to the south—was under the control of the Indians.

Just as the United States had not ventured across the Mississippi, leaving the Great Plains to the Indians, Argentina had not yet turned its face to the south. With independence, however, the new nation undertook to expel the Indians from the pampas. But the advance of settlement progressed hardly at all against the Indian challenge until the rise of Juan Manuel Rosas in the 1830s.

Rosas is a controversial figure in Argentine history, reviled and beloved. He was the first of the Argentine caudillos, a charismatic leader who for a time held absolute power. Rosas derived his power from his leadership of the emerging class of *estancieros,* who were establishing enormous land holdings to the south of Buenos Aires. Rosas himself was one of the largest landowners in Argentina; his principal *estancia,* or ranch, one of several on which he ran vast herds of cattle, comprised 300,000 hectares. It was only a matter of time before the expanding cattle industry clashed with the tribal economy of the pampas.

In the United States frontiersmen and smallholders led the way into the plains; in Argentina the military was the vanguard of the great landowners. At first, however, Rosas opposed the idea of military campaigns against the Indians, believing that constant warfare kept the Indians in a state of military preparedness. Appointed Commissioner of Indians in 1827, Rosas had a plan to bring peace to the frontier: create settlements along the border, establish military garrisons and create a buffer zone of Indians who were loyal to him and friendly to the state.

Rosas wooed the Indian leaders. He welcomed them to his estancia, offering gifts of cattle and horses. Rosas and Calfucura agreed to live in a state of peace in exchange for an annual shipment to the Indians of clothing, tobacco and eight thousand animals. Similar agreements with other important chiefs followed.

The agreements that Rosas struck with the tribes of the pampas were not treaties in the same sense as those signed in a similar period in North America: they were personal, negotiated man to man, caudillo to chief. They had no force in law, but they ensured that the chiefs remained loyal to Rosas, since he, and not the state, ensured that the promised supplies were delivered. During the Argentine Civil War of 1829–30, Rosas prevailed because his personal army included not only farm hands, the *gauchos,* but also Indian warriors. Rosas, like the Europeans in North America, found military alliances with the Indians useful.

After the Civil War, however, Rosas decided to march against the Indians, aiming to open new cattle country. Rosas undertook the Campaign of the Desert, a military drive against Indian tribes from Buenos Aires to the Rio Negro. In March 1833, he set off with a force of 1,500 men, 30 wagons, 6,000 horses and thousands of cattle. Charles Darwin, who caught sight of the expedition at the Rio Negro eight months later, was dismayed at the motley force of gauchos and vagabonds: "I should think such a villainous banditti-like army was never before collected together."

From the Rio Negro, Rosas's army marched eastward toward the Chilean border. He was lenient towards those tribes that were prepared to sign treaties with him; if they agreed to keep to the territory south of the Rio Negro, they were provided with rations and horses. On the other hand, Indians who remained defiant were treated harshly.

In the United States the country beyond the Mississippi was the country for the Indians. Beyond the Rio Negro, which more or less bisects Argentina from north to south, lay the Argentine version of Indian Country.

By the end of 1836, Rosas's campaign was ended. But it was by no means successful in evicting the Indians from the pampas. Tribes that had refused to negotiate treaties continued their raids on the estancias. The Indians who had agreed to stay beyond the Rio Negro often made their way back north across the river.

Argentina was not to undertake another campaign against the Indians for another generation. By then Argentina had passed the mid-century. In the sixty years since independence, Argentina had failed to consolidate the borders of the country. In 1850 there were fewer than a million Argentines; the Indians still disputed the nation's hold on the pampas; Patagonia was still in possession of the Indians. One Indian attack in 1876 penetrated to within sixty leagues of Buenos Aires, departing with 300,000 cattle and 500 White captives. To try to establish control, Argentina, in 1879, undertook a so-called Second Campaign of the Desert, led this time by General Julio Roca. Roca's campaign, he said, was a civilizing mission, intended to bring scientists and engineers to the frontier. Indeed, Roca's army of 6,000 troops was to have the most modern technology available, including four pieces of heavy artillery. In addition, Roca ordered the construction of the first telegraph lines into the countryside, so that his orders could be carried immediately to the front.

Roca believed in the manifest destiny of Argentina. As for the Indians, he told his troops:

> Destroying these nests of land-locked pirates and taking real possession of the vast region that surrounds you, you have opened the horizon of the homeland to the southern margins, mapping out with your bayonets an immense radius for its future development and grandeur.

Roca was aware that his campaign would take place almost simultaneously with the campaign by the United States against the Plains Indians. He went on:

> The United States, one of the most powerful nations of the earth, has not yet been able to solve the Indian question, despite trying a variety of methods, spending millions of dollars every year, and employing various armies. You, at the other end of the Americas, will solve the problem by your courage and your valour.

Roca emulated the tactics the United States Army used against the Indians of the plains. He made lightning raids against unsuspecting villages, killing or imprisoning the inhabitants, seeking to sow terror through the tribes of the pampas. The battles were bloody. Often the Indians realized that their lances were no match for the soldiers' rifles and "they threw their lances to the ground and began to fight with us hand to hand, to grab the rifles out of our grasp." Many of the hand-to-hand battles ended with soldiers on horseback trampling fleeing Indians.

The campaign, like its counterpart in North America, was successful. Roca systematically exterminated the Indians. Vast estancias were established on what novelist V. S. Naipaul has called the "stolen, bloody land." Many of the estancias were allotted to the victorious generals. Roca himself was rewarded with the presidency. Some of the Indians fled beyond the Rio Negro. Others were confined to concentration camps where measles became rampant among them, and countless of the captives died.

In the United States and Argentina, then, the conquest of the plains and the pampas was the means of establishing control over national boundaries and providing a national cause through which the populace could assert a common identity. In both countries the Indians fought desperately to defend their homelands and to survive.

What else was to be expected of them? To gracefully give up their tribal territories so as to come under the rule of invaders? Why should they have acknowledged the civilizing mission of the Whites, when White "civilization" deemed it right to appropriate the land of another people?

There is, however, one very important difference between the campaigns in the two countries and their aftermath. In the United States there was a legal structure and an established process, however inadequate, for treaties and for reservations. The rule of law, exemplified by the judgements of John Marshall, could not be ignored altogether. In Argentina, there was a statute in place that purported to recognize the rights of the Indians to land. Roca had no intention of abiding by it, however, and no civilian authority could call him to account. Furthermore, there was no civilian authority responsible for the welfare of the defeated remnants of the tribes. The military was predominant in Argentina then, as it has been so often since.

As a result, the Argentine government handled the shattered Native tribes in military fashion. The Indians who survived the war and the epidemic were given a choice: they could be settled in colonias where they would receive building materials, seeds and agricultural implements. Unlike the American reservations, where Indian identity survived in spite of appalling conditions, disease and starvation destroyed the Argentine Indian colonies within a generation. The other choice offered the Indians was assimilation. The Argentine military promoted a mass dispersal of able-bodied Indian men and women, who were sent off to become cheap labour in the towns and estancias. This hastened the extinction of any sense of Indian identity.

Argentines say that their history is one of martial glory and the opening of the frontier. But as Naipaul says, Argentina has "a simple history of Indian genocide and European takeover." According to Naipaul, even the great poet Jorge Luis Borges detested the memory of the Indians of the pampas, claiming that they could not even count.

Some will say that the experience of the United States and the experience of Argentina illustrate Europe's power to encompass the whole of the New World and the inevitability of its success in its drive to expel the Indians from their homelands. True it is that the Indians on horseback had only preceded the Europeans by a century in making the plains and the pampas their homeland. But possession, though it may not be nine points of the law, must count for something. The Indians used and occupied the land. Europe wanted it, and invaded it. No theory of a just war was called in aid, no mission to proselytise for Christ. Treaties were made in the United States and in Argentina, but without any intention of standing by them should it become expedient to repudiate them.

The ascendancy of Europe was now complete. These new American nation-states were not perched precariously on the water's edge, outnumbered by the Indians. No imperial government would call them to account. They no longer needed the Indians as allies. Their military power was, at the end of the day, overwhelming. All that was left in the United States was for those sympathetic to the Native cause to urge improvement of conditions on the reservations or to call for assimilation. In Argentina, no one was left to defend the Native cause, and soon very few Natives left to be defended. In Argentina the wars against the Indians led to virtual extinction of the erstwhile lords of the soil.

CHAPTER 8

Reserves, Reservations
and Reducciones

In January 1991, during a visit to Chile, I met with José Aylwin, whose father, Patricio Aylwin, is the first civilian president of Chile in the post-Pinochet era. José Aylwin is a member of the new civilian government's commission on human rights, which has special responsibility in relation to the rights of the Indians of the country. He told me that, as a result of legislation passed during the regime of General Augusto Pinochet, the Indians of Chile have lost 99 percent of their land. The means used were diabolically simple. The Chilean Indians have for many years lived on *reducciones indigenas,* or Indian reserves. Pinochet had the Chilean Congress pass a law providing that if one—only one—Indian member of the reserve wished to have the reserve subdivided into individual lots, it had to be done. In little more than a decade that followed passage of the law in 1979, of 2,000 Indian reserves in the country, 1,980 have been or are being subdivided. These small holdings cannot be sold for twenty years, but they can be leased. The individual plots of land are too small to be viable for agricultural purposes, so they are swiftly passing out of Indian control through long-term leases.

But such measures are not special to Chile. After the U.S. Indian Wars had ended, the Indians became wards of the United States government. War, disease and demoralization had overtaken them, rendering them helpless. Civilization was destined to triumph over savagery, and the Indians to disappear through death or assimilation. When the Indians still occupied the land beyond the Appalachians and west of the Mississippi, their constitutional position was acknowledged—it could be understood—there they were occupying Indian Country, geographically distinct. But when they were overrun and reduced to a remnant living in enclaves, dependent on federal generosity, it became easier to reject the notion that they ought to enjoy a distinct and special constitutional status. The Indians receded from the history of the American republic.

Some countries—Canada, the United States and Chile—have tried to dispose of the Indian question by establishing Indian reserves or reservations. These were places where Indian rule survived, on now diminished domains. But land has always been at the heart of the conflict between Europeans and Indians, and opposition between European and Indian ideas of land tenure remained, even with regard to these enclaves.

To the Indians, land is inalienable. Indians believe that land is held in common by all members of the tribe, a political community that is perpetual. Every member of the community in succeeding generations acquires an interest in the land as a birthright. In this way the tribal patrimony passes from one generation to the next. These ideas are not, however, widely understood or appreciated by Europeans. For them land is alienable, a commodity to be bought and sold; if land were inalienable this would impede its profitable use.

In the United States, following the Indian wars, the tribal reserves were surrounded by lands controlled by private landowners, by the states and territories or by the federal government. Americans rejected the Indian idea of communal ownership of land. Moreover, they rejected the idea that the tribes had the right to self-government on the lands they still held. The United States had become a great industrial power. To allow the Indians to continue to hold the land encompassed by the reservations and, what is more, to exercise governmental power over it, was thought of as contrary to all notions of progress. The Indian reservations still included valuable land—land that Whites wanted for settlement. From 1871, Congress adopted policies designed to put an end to tribal self-government and to extinguish their right to the remainder of their land.

Under the United States Constitution, treaties are entered into by the President with the advice and consent of the Senate. The House of Representatives was jealous of the power wielded by the President and the Senate. Furthermore, Congressmen resented the expenditure of federal revenues on Indians, believing that it encouraged them to live in idleness. The Senate joined the House in approving a rider to the *Appropriations Act* of 1871, which provided that Indians should no longer be "acknowledged or recognized as an independent tribe or power with whom the United States may contract by treaty."

Congress had decided there were to be no more treaties. But what now? The spirit of the age was exemplified by a Congressional Committee's declaration in 1871 of the virtues of private property. They said:

> No proposition is better established in the American mind than that the welfare of a state and happiness of its citizens require that the lands be held in private proprietorship, and in tracts sufficiently small that each may be cultivated and managed in person by its individual owners.

So Indian reserves should be broken up and allotted in individual parcels.

The federal government had first begun to experiment with dispersal of Indian lands by allotment in the 1850s. The idea was to divide the reservation lands into individual parcels or allotments. Tribal members would be given enough land to allow them to become farmers. The surplus remaining after individual allotments had been made would be opened up to White settlement. The proposal received support not only from those who were eager to obtain Indian lands but also from White people of good will, concerned by the invasion of Indian lands. The latter sympathized with the Indians but nevertheless favoured allotment, for they saw no future for the Indian way of life, regarding it as backward and condemned to extinction. The Indians' only hope, they believed, lay in adopting White ways and standards, in merging their lives and their land in the common stock.

The *General Allotment Act* of 1887, popularly known as the Dawes Act, after its champion in the Senate, Henry L. Dawes of Massachusetts, was the main legislative instrument to achieve the subdivision of reservation lands. Enacted along with a cluster of special allotment laws for individual tribes, this statute authorized the division of communally held reservations into individual parcels or allotments of sixty-four hectares for each Indian family head and thirty-two hectares to each single Indian over eighteen.

The Dawes Act was a firm rejection of tribal ownership of land. The Indians were to be made over into farmers, their land freely alienable. Moreover, when they severed their links with the tribe, the Indians would become citizens of the United States of America.

If the tribes were to be broken up, where would this leave the tribal governments? The tribes as such would be without a land base. What would there be left for them to govern? The answer was— nothing. This, too, was regarded as absolutely essential. Tribal governments were an anomaly in a progressive, democratic country.

Some reservations were not divided into allotments, and the land that remained from those that were divided was not always declared surplus and made available to settlers; in some cases, it remained in tribal ownership. Nevertheless, the Act's impact on Indian life and Indian land was enormous. In 1901, President Theodore Roosevelt declared that the *General Allotment Act* was "a mighty pulverizing engine to break up the tribal mass."

Under the Act the United States held each allotment in trust for the Indians for twenty-five years; during that time the land could not be sold, mortgaged or taxed. After twenty-five years, each Indian received a patent to the land. The land could then be sold, and could be taxed, and the Indian could become a United States citizen. By that time, it was hoped, the Indians would be prosperous farmers. That was the official theory. But, of course, it was understood, indeed explicitly acknowledged by most of those who wanted to gain possession of it, that the Indian land, once allotted, would inevitably pass from Indian ownership to White ownership.

Much of the allotted land was unsuitable for farming, and Congress never appropriated sufficient funds to enable Indians to buy farming equipment. Given the Indians' lack of capital, their lack of education, and the importuning of White purchasers, the scheme was bound to fail. By the 1920s, there was less land under cultivation by Indians than there had been at the time the Dawes Act was passed.

Two-thirds of all reservation lands were deeded to individual Indians. Nearly all of this land passed to non-Indian owners, often through state property tax foreclosures. Within fifty years, total Indian land holdings in the United States had been reduced from 55 million hectares to 19 million hectares. These statistics are, however, misleading, because the lands lost to the Indians were usually the most valuable lands they held.

Along with the assimilation of the land, the assimilation of the Indian people was not overlooked. The United States established boarding schools. Children were kept at school for years; every effort was made to remove them from the influence of their parents and tribes. Virtually everything Indian, including dress, language and religious practices, was banned. In Canada we did not adopt a *General Allotment Act,* but we did establish residential schools for Native children, institutions of forced assimilation operated by the churches, which scarred whole generations.

The *General Allotment Act* and related measures were intended to assimilate Indian land and the Indian people. To a great extent it succeeded in the former aim but not in the latter. Tribal life proved to be more durable than Congress anticipated. Tribal governments survived, though in attenuated form, and Indians continued to live on their shrunken reservation lands. The legislation did not bring about the assimilation of the Indians, because it did not take into account the basis of Indian cultural life—tribal identity.

Through all of these stages—removal, reservations, allotment and assimilation—the constitutional position of the Indian remained unchanged. In 1895, the Supreme Court of the United States held that Indian tribes were sovereign governments, not arms of the federal government. The language of the law did not, however, match the diminished reality on the ground.

With the election of President Franklin D. Roosevelt, a new policy for the Indians was adopted in an attempt to make tribal values and tribal lands secure. In 1934, Congress enacted the *Indian Reorganization Act* to halt further allotment of Indian reservations and to revitalize tribal governments. The loss of tribal lands came to an end.

Many Americans, however, now saw the future of Native Americans as citizens and workers in industrial America. The "peculiar institutions" of the Native people were out of keeping with notions of liberal democracy and debilitating to the Native people. An abortive policy of terminating Indian tribal status was adopted by Congress in 1953. Indian reserves were once again broken up and sold to the highest bidder.

Termination, like the allotment policy, did not work. The *General Allotment Act* had tried to remake Indians into farmers. In the 1950s they were to be relocated to the cities to become factory hands. This program, too, was a disaster. It destroyed nearly half a generation—and its legacy is the existence of Indian ghettos in urban centres. Unlike the allotment legislation of the nineteenth century, the termination legislation was never implemented on a national scale. After President John F. Kennedy came to office, his Secretary of the Interior, Stewart Udall, renounced any further attempts to implement the policy.

In recent years the legitimacy of the exercise of tribal government on Indian reservations has been affirmed by legislation as well as by a series of decisions of the Supreme Court of the United States during the same period. Powers exercisable by tribal governments now include the power to determine who is a member of the tribe, the power to tax, civil and criminal jurisdiction (including child welfare), regulatory authority over use of water, building codes, zoning, preferences for Native hiring and so on.

After 1933 the main current of United States legislation was intended to protect tribal governments and tribal lands. But this current did not flow into Alaska. Every attempt by Alaska Natives to obtain reservations was resisted: some were established, but very few. Land claims in that state went unacknowledged. Congress was not, however, through with its schemes of social engineering.

Another version of the *General Allotment Act* was adopted in Alaska, only this time the Natives were to give up their land to become businessmen. At each stage the United States wanted its Native population to adopt the current paradigm of progress: in 1887 it was farming, in the 1950s it was factory work, in 1971 it was business.

In 1971, when Congress passed the *Alaska Native Claims Settlement Act,* it set up a complicated scheme under which Native land—Indian, Eskimo and Aleut—would be held by Native corporations, in which the Natives would be shareholders. The ancestral land of the Native people would become an asset held by the corporations. Obviously, if the Native corporations fell under the control of non-Natives, Native land, a corporate asset, would pass effectively into the ownership of whomever acquired the shares of the corporation. So Congress decided that the Natives needed time to become successful businessmen. With this in mind, it was provided that the shares in the Native corporations could not be sold for twenty years. The Act was hailed as a model of its kind. Congress intended that the Native lands held by the Native corporations should be bought and sold like any other land.

Yet it did not work. In Alaska today, two decades after the enactment of the settlement, the net worth of the Native corporations is less than it was when they were established. They have not brought prosperity except to a few Natives and a very few communities. And Native people still believe it is necessary to retain their land in tribal ownership so that it will be passed on from generation to generation.

At the same time the state government of Alaska sought to integrate Natives into the political institutions of the state. The idea was that local municipal governments would replace tribal governments. Every inducement was offered to Native communities to adopt municipal government, every obstacle set in the way of tribal government. Yet this did not work either. Among Alaska Natives there has been a resurgence of support for tribal government.

As long as Native land in Alaska is in corporate ownership it can be lost through corporate takeovers, through foreclosure, or through sale. For two decades, ever since the passage of the statute, Alaska Natives have tried to persuade Congress to amend the legislation to thwart its main purpose, that is, they have sought to prevent their land passing from Native ownership. In 1988 Alaska Natives persuaded Congress to give them a further reprieve, through amendments to the Act. These amendments did not extend the period during which shares could not be sold, but they did make it exceptionally difficult to transfer shares. The amendments did not, however, meet the underlying concern of Alaska Natives for restoration of tribal ownership of Native land.

History demonstrates—and Alaska Natives know it—that there is a strong correlation between the loss of traditional lands and the marginalization of Native people. Without land, Native existence is deprived of its coherence and its distinctiveness. Today, Alaska Natives demand retribalization of Native land.

In 1979, Chile adopted the same failed policy the United States had tried in the lower forty-eight states in 1887 and again in Alaska in 1971; in Chile it was to prove ruthlessly effective.

The story of the Indian-White relations in Chile is chiefly the story of one Indian nation, the Araucanians, known in Chile as the Mapuche. The Mapuches are the most numerous Indian nation in Chile. In some of the southern provinces they make up, even today, a majority of the population. The Incas had not been able to conquer the Mapuches, and Spanish arms fared no better. After Chile gained its independence from Spain, its own troops also tried to subdue the Mapuches. For a long time they, too, were no more successful than the Spanish had been.

The Mapuches managed to retain most of their ancestral territory against Spanish and Chilean incursions for the best part of three hundred years. They waged continual guerilla warfare against the Spaniards. Until the late nineteenth century the southern boundary of European conquest in central Chile coincided with that of the Inca empire. Indeed the Mapuches were the most successful Indian tribe in the New World in resisting conquest by the Europeans.

After Chilean independence in 1818 there was an awakening of national interest in the colonization of Mapuche land. It was not until the latter years of the nineteenth century, however, that there was any deep penetration of Mapuche territory. That drive by Chilean forces in 1881 occurred almost simultaneously with Roca's onslaught against the Araucanians in Argentina. On either side of the Andes the Indians were in retreat.

In 1866 the Chilean government had established reservations, reducciones indigenas, for the Mapuches. Mapuche leaders were allowed to apply for large grants of land for themselves and their followers. At the same time, the law provided a mechanism for the division and dissolution of the reservation communities it created.

Meanwhile, all unclaimed land was to be sold to White settlers. In this the Chilean policy foreshadowed the *General Allotment Act*. The law resulted in the loss to the Mapuches of huge tracts of land. In fact it led to the last Mapuche Revolt, lasting two years, beginning in 1880. Once it was put down, the military power and political autonomy of the Mapuches had vanished.

After the final defeat of the Mapuches, the reducciones indigenas established in 1866 were further reduced in size, the expropriated land being used to enlarge the haciendas. The Mapuches, although restive under defeat and a harsh peace, were willing to accept the protection of the reservation system. They retained less than 500,000 hectares of the 10 million hectares they had held before the Mapuche wars. Unable to support themselves on their now diminished lands, the Mapuches became a migrant labour force on the haciendas; the reservations had become a reservoir of land and labour for the great landowners.

In the 1920s legislation was passed allowing for further division of the reservations, but it required assent by the community, though not necessarily by a majority. At the time of the armed forces coup in 1973 the Mapuches, numbering 500,000 on 2,000 reservations, were still clinging to an agricultural subsistence economy on their land, ekeing out a living as migrant labourers on the haciendas. But even this remnant of Mapuche communal life was an offence in the sight of the new regime.

On 12 September 1978, General Augusto Pinochet indicated what his government would do:

> This morning I wish to announce the promulgation in the near future of an act relating to indigenous property. This act, respecting the cultural values of the descendants of the Mapuche race, will enable those descendants voluntarily and freely to opt for private land ownership in those cases where they prefer this formula to the present system of community ownership.

In 1979 Pinochet's government introduced a law designed to divide the Mapuches' communally-held lands and turn them into small holdings. The law facilitated the breakup by providing that any one member of an Indian community could require that the land be divided. General Pinochet explained that "such communities are incompatible with the Nation's economic progress." There was bound to be at least one Indian on each reservation who could be persuaded to agree with General Pinochet.

The draft version of the 1979 law provided that once land was divided among the Indians, the Indian landholders would no longer be considered to be Indians. After protests by the Catholic Church this clause was deleted; it was a perfectly honest statement, however, of the true purpose of the statute. It was intended to put an end to Indian land tenure and Indian identity. Today only twenty Mapuche reservations remain intact. The new civilian government has agreed to enact a law to stop any further division, but given the drastic loss of land already incurred, this is more symbolism than anything else.

As for those Indians who acquired land, the parcels were too small—only five hectares—to enable them to farm efficiently. The Chilean statute, perhaps in imitation of the Alaska limitation on the sale of shares, provided that the Indians could not sell their individual parcels of land for twenty years. There was, however, no prohibition on leasing the land. So, most of the Mapuches have leased their small plots of land for ninety-nine years to Whites who were already farming in contiguous areas or who wanted to acquire rural recreational land. The loss of their birthright is a violation of collective human rights that for the Mapuche is a tragedy beyond measure, perhaps beyond remedy.

Why were these measures passed in both North and South America? Granted, in the United States at the time of the Dawes Act and in Chile in 1979 there were local speculators who wished to obtain Indian lands. Nevertheless, the primary impetus was ideological or philosophical, exemplified by Theodore Roosevelt's determination "to break up the tribal mass" or General Pinochet's declaration that the Indians' communal ownership of land was "incompatible with the Nation's economic progress." Not for them any consideration of tribal tradition—except to destroy it; not, indeed, any consideration of the utility of communal land tenure for purposes of local land management. It was the idea of progress in the form of individual ownership of land, of the destiny of the White landowner to acquire the Indians' land, that excluded any notion of Indian forms of land tenure.

To advocate communal ownership of Native lands is not a matter of allowing Native people to remain attached to an outmoded form of land tenure. Idealogues of the right, believing in the marketplace, argue that all land should be divided into private holdings. They distrust any deviation from a comprehensive regime of private tenure. Ideologues of the left believe that only government is capable of developing resources efficiently and fairly. Suppression of indigenous people's land tenure arrangements is also the norm in countries where Marxist regimes have been established. Marxism, like capitalism, is a European ideology which sees no place for indigenous peoples' forms of land tenure. In Nicaragua the Sandinista government's treatment of the Miskito Indians and other tribes, certainly in the regime's early years, exemplified this tendency. In 1972, in Chile, the socialist government of Salvador Allende enacted a statute that was an exception to the rule. It was intended to restore lost lands to the Mapuches. Under the statute 68,381 hectares were returned to the Mapuches. This brief "spring" was ended by the advent of the Pinochet regime.

Ideology has blinkered us. Common property may be viable on grounds of both efficiency and equity. Rather than representing an atavistic arrangement of rights which inevitably results in inefficient resource use, it may be the best way to manage certain resources. And not only in Latin America, where communal land tenure has been the predominant form of tenure in the tropical forests, but in North America as well. As Native land claims move forward in the forested provinces of Canada, such as British Columbia, may we not find that local communal land tenure provides local control and management that looks to the long term, to the next generation as well as next week?

The measures we have taken since 1492 have been designed to ensure that Indian land passed into European ownership, whether that of individuals or of the state. The colonies of Europeans established throughout North and South America—and the nation-states that succeeded them—adopted legal regimes to achieve this. The only feature of these regimes that worked to protect Indian land tenure was the prohibition on the sale of land by Indians to private individuals like that found in the Royal Proclamation of 1763. The *General Allotment Act,* the *Alaska Native Claims Settlement Act* and their Chilean counterparts were specifically designed to get around this prohibition.

Are Native people ever to be secure in the possession of what land remains to them? Are they, wherever they live in the lands that once were theirs, to have the right to control their own lives? The question of the future of the Indian people and their claims to restoration of ancestral lands ought to trouble even the most shrunken of national consciences.

CHAPTER 9

Guatemala: Rebirth
of the Black Legend

In December 1989 I was asked to represent a Guatemalan refugee, whose name need not be mentioned here, seeking to enter Canada. He had fled his own country because in Guatemala he had been assisting a Roman Catholic priest working among the Indians. Priests and other ordinary people like my client who helped the Indians and the poor were persecuted by the Guatemalan military. The military had shot and beaten my client and left him for dead. I was engaged by the immigration lawyers of British Columbia, who wished to see refugees provided with the means to retain counsel, to try to obtain a court order requiring the province's Legal Aid Society to pay for legal representation for my client. It was a test case, and we were successful. The Supreme Court of British Columbia ordered the Legal Aid Society to provide legal aid; as a result, in the first twelve months after the judgement, legal aid was provided to more than two thousand refugees entering Canada at Vancouver; in April 1991, the British Columbia Court of Appeal upheld the order of the lower court. My client has since been admitted to Canada as a landed immigrant.

This brief encounter with victims of Guatemalan violence has been repeated throughout Canada. Lawyers, churches and others have aided them. My assignment gave me an insight into one man's suffering under a contemporary regime whose violence towards the Indians of Guatemala bears a close resemblance to that instituted five hundred years before that won for Spain's dispensation in the Americas the name of the Black Legend.

The United States was not eager to admit refugees from Central American countries such as Guatemala and El Salvador, with right wing governments, for the reason that since these were democracies their citizens could have no well-grounded fear of persecution and death. It was, however, prepared to open its doors to refugees from Nicaragua. Canada was willing to receive refugees from all these countries. Canada's refugee determination procedure is difficult to negotiate, but it is nevertheless easier than that of the United States. As a result refugees flocked from Guatemala to Canada. Indeed, Canada has been a haven for refugees for many years. Today it has the highest per capita number of refugees of any country in the world.

Guatemala is one of Latin America's Potemkin democracies. In the Orwellian world the United States has created in Central America, the election of a president of the right political stamp stands as proof of the advent of democracy and the rule of law. In Guatemala, however, presidents may govern but the military are the true rulers.

It was in Guatemala in the sixteenth century that Bartolomé de Las Casas established the colony of Verapaz where Spaniards and Indians were to live together in harmony. Today in Guatemala the military have obliterated Las Casas's dream of a land of true peace.

The Indians of Guatemala are descendants of the great Maya civilization. Today they number twenty-two tribes or nations, living in the country's highlands, engaged in subsistence agriculture. Each of the tribes has a distinct language, customs and dress, each a separate territory.

These rural Indian communities are the seat of Native culture and tradition; in these communities the Native identity has been as firmly maintained as anywhere in the New World. In recent years, however, they have been the victims of a war waged by the conquistadores' successors against the Indian population of Guatemala. This massacre has taken place in North America's backyard, yet it is one we have hardly noticed.

Each of the Central American countries has had its fifteen minutes under the United States media spotlight: El Salvador, then Nicaragua. Events in these countries have been seen in the context of the struggle between U.S.-sponsored governments or U.S.-sponsored guerillas acting out their small parts on the Cold War stage. Even Panama had its moment of fame, when the United States kidnapped the dictator it had earlier sponsored.

We do hear occasionally of controversies over human rights in Guatemala, and of conflicts between the landowners, the military and the radicals. The assassination of lawyers, priests and politicians arouses genuine but short-lived concern in Canada, the United States and other countries.

It makes a kind of sense to us: here are the great landowners and their military protectors, here the middle class, there the urban reformers, in the bush the guerillas, many lives at risk. All of this we can comprehend. But we cannot comprehend the wholesale destruction of Indian villages, the murder of tens of thousands of Indians carried out for no apparent purpose. The Guatemalan army has undertaken a crusade to assassinate its own countrymen in the name of anti-Communism. This cry is especially ludicrous, for nowhere in the New World have Indian people been persuaded to march as a monolithic entity under the banner of Communism, or any other European ideology, for that matter.

This slaughter of a rural people is in its own way comparable to Stalin's enforced starvation of millions in the Ukraine in the 1930s or to Pol Pot's deliberate destruction of one-third of the people of Cambodia in the 1970s. Yet it has been virtually ignored by Western media and by Western governments. Tens of thousands of Indians exterminated, villagers in the highlands forced to kill their kin, a Final Solution to the Indian problem devised by crackpot military commanders, an attempt by Guatemalans to deny their own Indian blood by extinguishing its living embodiment.

In all of Latin America, no people has been more profoundly affected by state terror than the Indian people of Guatemala. Nowhere in Latin America have the abuses of human rights been as dreadful as in Guatemala. It has truly been the Black Legend revisited.

> The [soldiers] searched the houses and pulled the people out and took us to a churchyard. The Lieutenant walked up and down pointing at people, saying, "These will go to hell, these will go to heaven." The ones he said would go to hell they took . . . to the cemetery with their hands tied behind their backs. They dug a big ditch and lined them up at the edge. We all had to come and watch. . . . They shot each one with a bullet in the face from about a meter away.

This is just one eyewitness account among hundreds that have been collected by observers visiting the refugee camps along the border that divides Mexico from Guatemala. These camps have offered shelter to more than 150,000 refugees escaping from the terror of the Guatemalan army. The refugees have described a wave of murder and mutilation: wives forced to witness the interrogation and torture of their husbands; parents watching, helplessly, as their children are hacked to death with machetes. The populations of entire villages have been annihilated, the bodies dumped in common graves.

The human rights organization Americas Watch estimates that, since the 1960s, the Guatemalan military has been responsible for more than one hundred thousand deaths. Many of these victims are White or mestizo citizens who have spoken out against the regime. Others are union organizers, student leaders, journalists. But the greatest number of the victims are Indians.

What possible justification is there for an army—one that has rarely fired a shot at an alien enemy—to wage a savage war against its own helpless citizenry? And why have Indians borne the brunt of the terror?

The wars of independence in Central America were imitative of the American War of Independence. Each of the new nations adopted a constitution copied from that of the United States. But they were seldom true democracies. Wealth remained in the hands of a few. Those few modelled themselves on Europe. These Central American oligarchies, aping the cultures of Europe, may seem absurd, but increasingly they spawned a breed of military strongmen, crafty though often ignorant, whose bullying populism has sometimes won them the support of the people. Usually, however, the Indians failed to join in the vicarious celebration of power. In any event none of these regimes acknowledged any significant place for the Indians as collectivities. Indeed, the continued existence of the Indians was a reminder to these elites of their counterfeit culture, the suspect character of their blood-lines.

In North America, under the influence of John Marshall, the Indian tribes were understood to be nations, their tribal governments viable political institutions exercising limited sovereignty, entitled to powers of self-government that derived from their aboriginal occupation of the land. It will be said, this is all very well in the United States and, it may be, in Canada as well, where Indian populations are small and marginal. We can adopt such a theory of Indian sovereignty without undermining the sovereignty of the nation-state. But many of the Latin American countries have large Indian populations, so they are unwilling to acknowledge that Indian political institutions can be a part of a modern political system.

In Mexico and Peru, where the pattern of Latin American settlement was established, the Spaniards assumed control over vast Indian populations and intermarried with them. The mestizo population is the result of these unions. New governments were constructed on the basis that there was one central regime and one people. Many Indians did become acculturated and came to regard themselves as European. But substantial Indian populations remained, without any distinctive place in the new political system. Today in Guatemala Indians still outnumber Whites and mestizos.

After independence was achieved in Latin America, conditions became even worse for the Indians. The settlers were now free of the restraints imposed by Spain. Even the liberals were usually out of sympathy with the Indian way of life. They regarded programs to maintain the lands and customs of the Indians as inimical to Indian well-being, for they checked the development in the Indians of a capitalist spirit of enterprise and initiative. Even great heroes of Indian birth, such as Benito Juárez, president of Mexico and a reformer, rejected the concept of an Indian identity, insisting that Indians must cease to be Indians and become Mexicans.

In some countries, such as El Salvador, Indians have been forcibly acculturated. In 1932 Indians in that country engaged in an uprising to regain their communal lands and to re-establish their tribal governments. The military government ordered troops to shoot every man in Indian dress. Thirty thousand Indians died. In that country, it has often been said by the regime, there are no Indians. But this is the exception, not the rule. Mexico has perhaps 20 million people who are Indians and regard themselves as Indians. In Ecuador, Peru and Bolivia there are six million Indians. These peoples live culturally apart from the dominant peoples of European descent. Yet, as collectivities, they have no rights to speak of.

The Latin American oligarchies are aware of the vast Indian populations surviving in their midst. Yet they believe that to acknowledge their claims, to accept their right as peoples to a measure of autonomy, would undermine the fragile European regimes. So they cling to a pretence that all people are merely citizens of one nation-state, with no loyalties except to the state. If there are Indians, then they are on their way to assimilation, or ought to be. But assimilation has not taken place in five hundred years, and it will not come about today except forcibly, as it did in El Salvador.

In Guatemala the culture of the Indians has exhibited very great resilience; Indian communal values enabled them to survive despite domination. As a result, five centuries after the Conquest, Guatemala is unique among the countries of Central America: the majority of the population is of Indian heritage and culture, the Native languages are still widely spoken and the traditional communities survive.

But Guatemala has always been a land of inequality, inequality guarded by military strongmen. The rich landowners have always held the fertile lowlands—a fraction of the populace owned nearly three-quarters of the arable land. The Indians of the highlands eked out a meagre living by travelling to the hot lowlands along the coast during the harvest to work on the sugar, coffee and cotton plantations under dreadful conditions.

In 1944 a junta of conservative generals was overthrown by progressive officers and cadets. A new constitution was drawn up. In 1945 Guatemalans elected a government determined to ameliorate the stunning inequities in the country's social and economic life. During a period that has become known as "ten years of spring" two reform administrations attempted for the first time since the Spanish conquest to alter the social and economic structure of the country. They undertook a program of agrarian reform, which had the effect of turning the wealthy landowners of Guatemala into the unforgiving enemy of the Indian majority. Only 16 percent of Guatemala's privately owned arable land was ever taken over, but 100,000 peasant families received land. Altogether perhaps 500,000 people, most of them Indian, gained by land reform. Although compensation was provided for the lands that had been expropriated, the landowners were determined to regain the land awarded to the Indians.

In 1954, the U.S. Central Intelligence Agency organized a successful military coup against the president, Jacobo Arbenz. The oligarchy and their military protectors were restored, and land reform was rolled back. The military began rounding up Indians in the mountain villages and transporting them to the plantations on the coast to serve once again as a labour force on the plantations.

With the crushing of the reform movement in Guatemala, disaffected military officers, seeking to emulate the success of Fidel Castro in Cuba, established small guerilla forces in remote areas of the mountains inhabited only by isolated groups of Indian peasants. These guerillas were unable to recruit the local Indian populace to their cause, because the Indians' profound mistrust of the Whites and mestizos extended even to them. This first phase of guerilla activity soon petered out.

In Washington and Guatemala City, however, the guerilla activity stimulated a military response far beyond that warranted by guerilla numbers. Guatemala entered a new period of military rule, darker than any since the Conquest. At first, the armed forces were intent on consolidating their military strength by quelling any movement that seemed to threaten the power of the state and the established order of wealth. But after that the armed forces became synonymous with the state, dominating the nation not only politically but also economically.

The rise of military regimes in Guatemala since the 1950s, and especially in the 1970s and 1980s, has reduced Indian land holdings and gone very far toward destroying the social and economic structure of their communities. Their traditional social and economic arrangements, which have since the time of the Conquest promoted community solidarity, have for this very reason been considered suspect.

In Guatemala, the story of the conquistadores—soldiers who became landowners—is repeating itself. The Guatemalan army's officers are White and mestizo, its conscripts Indians. More so than in any other Latin American country, in Guatemala the officer class has become the new ruling class. The armed forces not only hold state power but they also control sizeable sectors of the economy.

All forms of dissent, all opposition, the Guatemalan military treats as a threat to the nation, punishable at the arbitrary choice of the military and often by death. The result has been the growth of state terror: kidnapping, torture, disappearances and death.

The Guatemalan military, with American encouragement, was determined to keep Guatemala in the free world, no matter how unfree its people's condition. Guatemalan officers thought of themselves as defenders of Christian civilization against a communist takeover. In 1970 the armed forces took political control of the country, ostensibly so that the military could purge corruption from the political parties. All potential sources of dissent—universities, political parties and the Catholic Church—were treated as suspect. Death squads began targeting leaders of liberal political parties, trade unions and peasant co-operatives. Members of the death squads, many of whom were off-duty police or military officers, enjoyed immunity from prosecution.

Over the following two decades Guatemala has been run by a succession of generals. In fact the years following 1978 became known in the country as the "decade of the generals"—the regimes of General Fernando Lucas García, General Efraín Rios Montt and General Mejias Victores. In 1978, after General Lucas García assumed power, kidnapping and assassination of political opponents became endemic. The death squads became an extension of the armed forces. Violence against civilians was organized from military headquarters. What had been terror by private death squads countenanced by those in power, became the official policy of the state. Kidnappings, once selective, now became random, a means of mass repression.

Death squads moved their headquarters to military bases throughout the country. The war in the cities moved to the countryside. The campaign of terror bore with unique savagery on the Indians. In the cities individuals were targeted, but in the countryside whole villages were targeted.

The rise of the generals coincided with the growth of organizations designed to give Guatemalans, and particularly poor Guatemalans, a collective voice in national affairs. In the 1970s the Catholic Church began to organize rural co-operatives, linking peasants from various parts of the country in a single organization. Some of the goals of the co-operative movement were practical: to improve access to seed, fertilizers and markets. They also, however, were the means for Indian peasants to press for social and economic changes across the country.

These peasant organizations were bound to come into direct conflict with the armed forces. The military were not only guardians of the established oligarchy; they had themselves become the oligarchy, had taken control of the economy. During the 1970s, the generals made several important financial accords with some of the largest of the North American mining and petroleum firms. The increase in investment from abroad allowed the armed forces to establish the Army Bank, now one of the great financial institutions in the country.

The military had become supreme, without any restraints on its freedom of action. Three notable atrocities occurred that illustrate the determination of the military to defend the new political and economic order.

In northern Guatemala, a development corridor, the Franja Transversal del Norte, was carved out of an isolated territory that is the homeland of the Kekchi and Ixil Indians. Many of the agribusinesses along the corridor are owned by senior members of the armed forces; these estates together are known as "The Zone of Generals." In May 1978, the Indians who were displaced by the generals staged a march on the city of Panzos. Seven hundred Indian peasants carried a letter to the mayor, demanding restoration of their lands. As they reached the town square, government forces and local vigilantes positioned on the roofs of buildings around the square fired on the throng. More than one hundred Indians were killed within minutes, and more died trying to escape the massacre. Their bodies were buried in mass graves that had been prepared by bulldozers the day before.

In January 1979, a group of Indian organizers travelled to Guatemala City to protest the widespread violence against Indian peasants in the countryside. In an attempt to focus international attention on the problem, they occupied the Spanish Embassy and demanded to speak with the ambassador, an outspoken critic of human rights violations committed by the Guatemalan military against Spanish priests and their parishioners. While the delegation was conferring with the ambassador, the Guatemalan army surrounded the embassy. Despite pleas from the ambassador, who reminded the military that his embassy was Spanish territory, the military smashed its way in and opened fire, engulfing the building in flames. All but one of the peasants died.

Then there was the first national strike of rural labourers. An organizing drive throughout the 1970s culminated in May 1978 when all of the peasant organizations of the country joined forces for the first time. In 1980, 75,000 workers on the sugar, coffee and cotton plantations along the southern coast of the country staged a fifteen-day strike, demanding an increase in wages. The strike ended with a substantial wage increase. But the victory by strike action led nowhere. Landowners simply refused to honour the new wage agreements, and nothing was done to compel them to do so.

The Panzos massacre of 1978 demonstrated to Indians everywhere in the country that there was no official recourse to protect their villages and their traditional land base against the military's new economic hegemony. The strike on the south coast illustrated that the government could not or would not require the landowners to honour their contracts. And the massacre at the Spanish Embassy illustrated that the Guatemalan military was deaf to international protest.

In the late 1970s, a new wave of guerilla activity began in the isolated areas of northern Guatemala. Guerillas began organizing in remote areas populated only by Indians. The Indians came to sympathize with the aims of the guerilla organizations. By the 1980s there were an estimated 5,000 active guerillas and perhaps 250,000 Indian sympathizers.

The reaction of the military was to isolate Indians and Indian villages suspected of aiding the guerillas. The torture chambers that had been established in urban centres were now set up in villages in the mountains—in clinics, in schools and in churches. Indian peasants were rounded up at random and ordered to inform on any villagers who were thought to be sympathetic to the guerillas.

As the repression deepened, the selective killings in the rural areas became massacres in which entire villages were annihilated. Soldiers entered villages, usually by night, and fired on all of the inhabitants. The Guatemalan military treated the Indian villagers as an undifferentiated mass, any one of whom might be the enemy.

To escape this tyranny, some Indians—individuals, families and the populations of entire villages—fled to Chiapas in Mexico, Bartolomé de Las Casas's old bishopric. Yet at the time the world paid more attention to the Palestinian refugees in the Gaza or the Afghan refugees in Pakistan. These were conflicts arising from age-old Middle Eastern animosities or East-West rivalry that we could understand, conflicts that we have been conditioned to regard as bearing, even though distantly, on our own welfare. But the catastrophe visited on the highland peoples of Guatemala—indigenous peoples living in our own hemisphere—*never* became a subject of national attention in the United States or Canada.

Those villagers who did not choose to leave Guatemala escaped into the mountains and became internal refugees, cultivating new lands for their crops where they hoped they would not be discovered. There may have been as many as one million of these internal refugees. To the army, the refugee communities in the mountains were indistinguishable from guerilla bases. The army gave the Indians who had escaped to the mountains a choice: they could be relocated in camps next to army posts, or they would be shot. Soldiers made forays to search out these new refugee communities and to force those who had fled to move to army camps. Those who escaped were hunted down. Those suspected of sympathizing with or supporting the guerillas were massacred.

One witness interviewed by Americas Watch described the army assault on her village in the following way.

> I was sitting down with my children—with my babies—everyone was there in the house. And all of a sudden I saw them come in, surround the house . . . [W]hen my 16 year old son got up—my baby—as soon as I looked at him, they shot him. . . . They shot him in the knee but when I came over, they brought the machete and they finished him off with the machete. They cut his throat. . . . And my other child, my daughter, she was bathing. She was bathing and wearing only her shawl; she was in the river near a ravine. . . . And when I ar-

rived there, there she was; there was my daughter hanged in the place where she had been washing herself.

On 18 April 1982, soldiers came to the village of Chiapac, and told the villagers to assemble in the church:

> The people were surrounded and could not leave the church. Then the soldiers called out people's names, including children, and took them to the clinic nearby. All the names were of people who had learned to read and write. . . .
> The women were raped before the eyes of the men and the children in the clinic. The men and the boys had their testicles cut off. Everybody's tongues were cut out. Their eyes were gouged out with nails. Their arms were twisted off. Their legs were cut off. The little girls were raped and tortured. The women had their breasts cut off. . . .

It was not an accident that this atrocity began in a church. There is a strong anticlerical element to the military repression in Guatemala because in recent years the Catholic Church has spoken out in defence of human rights in Guatemala. Priests were killed, many more fled the country.

Villagers who moved to the army camps were resettled in makeshift communities. These "model villages" are administered directly by the military. In these camps shelter consists of tin-roofed, one-room shanties. Food is rationed. Water must be carried from a central tap and sanitation is primitive. The Indians must attend lectures against subversion given by the military. All camp residents practise military manoeuvres on the parade ground.

The statistics are appalling. By the end of 1984, in northern Quiché, there were 60,000 displaced persons out of a total population of 82,000. Nine "model villages" had been built to replace forty-nine destroyed communities.

Such camps strike at the fundamental organization of Indian life. Indians from villages distant from one another are thrown together. Ancestral polities are dismembered. Cultural traditions are jumbled in the throng.

Everyone who visited Guatemala used to speak or write about the costumes distinctive to each village. Wherever Indians went they

wore their distinctive village dress. This was the outward manifestation of Indian identity, of attachment to local tradition, of a consciousness of local history stretching back long years before the
establishment of Guatemala or even the coming of the Spanish. As
Rigoberta Menchú has written, each village has its own traditions, its
own secrets.

Today the wearing of distinctive village dress is a liability. The
model villages are a mechanism for breaking up the links between
the Maya, for establishing a new order that will constitute a complete break with Mayan communal solidarity. The terror is intended
to complete at last the destruction of Mayan identity begun by the
conquistadores.

The conquistadores had to incorporate the Indians into a new political and economic order. The outnumbered Spanish had to subdue
the Indians by force and terror. At an atavistic level the Guatemalan
military has assumed the same task today.

Perhaps the most monstrous feature of the Guatemalan army's
totalitarian regime in the highlands is the Civil Action Patrol, established in the early 1980s to ensure that Indian communities did not
provide support for the guerilla forces. The Army set out to form
civilian brigades to patrol all of the highland villages. The Civil Patrollers are supposed to guard the villages. But they are also used as
cannon fodder in skirmishes with the guerillas.

The military has required the enforced co-operation of almost all
of the highland population, including old men, boys and women. In
1982, when the government of General Rios Montt first announced
the formation of the Civil Patrol, it included 25,000 civilians; eighteen months later the number had increased to 700,000. Within two
years, over a million men, women and children, had been coerced
into participation in an organization ostensibly aimed at the eradica-
tion of 5,000 guerillas.

The Civil Patrol is in truth a vast apparatus for civilian sur-
veillance and control; patrollers are expected to turn over to the
military anyone whom they suspect of harbouring subversive sym-
pathies. This has caused deep, perhaps irreconcilable, divisions
within Indian communities. The patrols are sent out to sweep the
surrounding mountains for Indian families who may have gone into
hiding and to kill them. The following story illustrates how the patrols have been used to destroy the spirit of an entire village:

He told me that the army had come to his village and pre-sented five men from the same village to the people there. They were prisoners. The villagers knew the men, they were their neighbours. The army commander told the people that they were guerillas and the civil patrol must "decide" what to do with them: they could kill them—that was their "business"—or they could let them go free. The army said it would return to see what their decision had been.

The civil patrol did not know what to do. . . . They were very upset, they knew their neighbours were not guerillas. And all this time, while they were deciding what to do, the five men were standing there, beside them, listening. . . . They came to a community decision to kill their neighbours because "if we don't kill you, the army will come back and massacre the entire village. . . .

Everyone in the village lined up and hugged the condemned men goodbye and they begged them for forgiveness. They asked the men to understand that they did it only for the good of the entire village, and that it was better for five to die than for the entire community to be massacred afterwards. . . . The men shot the five. To their surprise, the army showed up mo-ments after the killing; they had hidden nearby to see what the people would do. That day there were five new widows and eighteen fatherless children in that community.

These harrowing tales remind us of the atrocities that accompa-nied the Conquest. The same savagery, the same disregard for the value of Indian life. In five hundred years nothing has changed for the Mayas, except that the likelihood of their survival as a distinct people is perhaps more perilous than ever before. This is not to say that the guerillas have not been guilty of acts of savagery against In-dians. But the military campaign against the Indians is so far-reaching, pervasive and malignant that it amounts to genocide.

The word genocide is often used indiscriminately, but it can fairly be applied to what has happened in Guatemala. It is a violation of the Genocide Convention of 1948 to commit any of the following acts "with the intent to destroy, in whole or in part, a national, ethnical, racial or religious group, as such: (a) killing members of the group; (b) causing serious bodily or mental harm to the group; (c) deliberately inflicting on the group conditions of life calculated to bring about its physical destruction in whole or in part. . . . " The Guatemalan military may be said to be guilty on all counts.

Elections were held in Guatemala in 1985. A civilian president was elected but was powerless to govern. The military still ruled in the highlands. Yet this charade of popular democracy was hailed in the United States. In 1991, still another civilian president was elected. Like his predecessor, he is bound to give a free hand to the military in the war against the guerillas, in truth, a war against the Indians.

Why has Guatemala countenanced this terror against the indigenous peoples of the highlands? In the guise of anti-Communism it has found a way to eliminate a very different type of collectivity which has threatened the fragile nation-states of the region since the days of the conquistadores. It is a means of eradicating Native culture, of enforcing the European idea of progress in its misshapen Guatemalan form, an idea the advance of which is impeded by the survival of Indian culture and of the Indians themselves. If Indian identity cannot be eliminated by assimilation then it must be done by force and intimidation. What of the guerillas? They do not necessarily believe that the struggle is pre-eminently an Indian struggle. They prefer to cast it in terms of class struggle and land reform, on behalf of the poor and oppressed of Guatemala, not as a campaign to ensure the survival of the Indian nations within Guatemala.

Despite the depredations of state terror the Indian nations still exist in Guatemala. They have been despoiled of their lands, often of their dignity. But they are not willing to vanish into the mass of Latin American poverty. Ronald Wright has written that "Guatemala is a white settler colony masquerading as a nation. . . . " Until Guatemala acknowledges that Indian land, Indian culture and Indian survival, and the refusal by Guatemalans to recognize their legitimacy, lie at the heart of the nation's trauma, there will be no resolution of the political and economic sickness that has afflicted the country for five centuries.

CHAPTER 10

The Last Redoubt:
The Survival of Subsistence

In 1985, after I had completed my report on the *Alaska Native Claims Settlement Act,* I was testifying in support of my recommendations for changes to the Act before the Interior Committee of the United States House of Representatives. When I talked about the importance of hunting and fishing to Alaska Natives, about what Alaska Natives call the subsistence economy or subsistence, Congressman John Sieberling said to me,

> That's all very well, but how are we to bring Native people into the modern world?

I tried to explain—how successful I was, I do not know—that in the Arctic and sub-Arctic regions of North America subsistence hunting and fishing is actually a part of the modern world. In these regions, until recently, Native land was not coveted. Here the traditional economy of Native people has not been extinguished. They still occupy the land and use it as before—for hunting and fishing and trapping for fur. In many places in North America the subsistence economy is still important to Native people, but this is especially so for the Native people of the Arctic and sub-Arctic in Canada and the United States.

Even in these remote regions, however, the subsistence economy is under attack. Wherever, at the frontier, the search goes on for oil, gas and minerals, Native lands are at risk, the subsistence economy under siege. Even people who do not want or need Native land do not understand the subsistence economy or its importance. As a result, Native people are obliged to defend the *idea* of subsistence itself.

Of course, to maintain the subsistence economy, Native people seek to preserve fish and wildlife populations, and this entails working to protect the environment. Native people have allies who, like them, urge the protection of wilderness and wildlife. But although their allies in the environmental movement believe in wilderness and wildlife, they do not always believe in the subsistence economy.

To Native people wilderness and wildlife are essential to their survival, for upon them depends the subsistence way of life. To us, however, subsistence is an anachronism; it evokes an image of living at the edge of starvation. Yet it has always been the way of life of Native peoples in the Arctic and sub-Arctic, and today many Native villages still depend upon it.

We tend to think of the history of the last five hundred years as the history of the triumph throughout the world of European science and technology. We regard our world as an industrial world— one conceived by science and built by technology. Those persons who represent the industrial system have a complete and entire commitment to it, as a way of life and as a source of income. This is so whether they are public servants, representing governments dedicated to economic growth and expansion, or executives and workers in the mining or oil and gas industries, whose lives are devoted to the same goals. Or even environmentalists, who seek to maintain natural oases in the midst of the works of industrial man. Subsistence is considered to be the antithesis of modernity.

The Arctic and sub-Arctic regions of North America are the current battleground over subsistence. Although the Arctic and sub-Arctic are not suitable for agriculture, White people have always regarded them as lands rich in resources: first furs, then gold and other minerals and now oil and gas.

The White man still wishes to conquer the frozen and waste spaces, to build roads, mines, drilling rigs, oil and gas wells and pipelines. He dreams of the technological conquest of the northern frontier, a place that is considered barren, inhospitable to humankind.

We thought of the early explorers of the Arctic and sub-Arctic as if they were tracing their way across some far-off planet. We thought of them as the first cartographers of the Arctic. In Canada we now know, through recent Native mapping projects, that before Europeans came the North was already mapped in Native people's minds—traced all over by their hunting patterns.

Even today we read accounts of the early exploration and navigation of the Arctic as if the region had been uninhabited, like Antarctica, and its exploration nothing more than a challenge to European courage, endurance and technology. To chroniclers of exploration by sea the Inuit were faceless people peeping through the icebergs. Even to those who came by land, guided by Indians of the northern forest, the skills of the Natives were not regarded as essential to the task of exploration. Yet in the North, as throughout the Americas, the Europeans encountered people with their own history, their own culture and their own technology.

The advent of Whites in the North was spearheaded by explorers seeking to extend the fur trade. The clergy followed, to provide salvation and schooling; then came representatives of government. In this the North reflects the pattern of historical development arrived in frontier in North America. But this is a frontier like no other.

When the prairies were opened up by the railways, it meant the coming of agricultural settlement, the establishment of centres of White population and widespread diffusion of European languages and culture. In the North, however, given its climate and soil conditions, agricultural settlement throughout most of the area is out of the question: you cannot grow wheat on the tundra. Its non-renewable resources—gold, silver, lead, zinc, copper, uranium and oil and natural gas—provide the main thrust of economic development.

It was not until this century that we decided we needed the mineral resources of the North. So this comparatively recent onslaught has been rather more benign—seen through our own eyes—than the march across the plains and the pampas a century ago.

Alaska has 70,000 Eskimos, Indians and Aleuts. In Canada, 30,000 Dene, Metis and Inuit live north of the 60th Parallel. In Greenland, there are 50,000 Inuit. These are small populations, yet in the North they are significant. In many areas they are virtually the only permanent residents. For most of the government employees, teachers, miners and workers on the drilling rigs, the North is a place to work but not to stay a lifetime.

The Native people of the North have lived off the land for centuries. Change came with the advent of the fur trade, as they became partners in a new kind of economy, but one based on traditional activities—hunting, fishing and trapping—albeit with rifles and equipment obtained through trading in furs.

When, however, the whole apparatus of government arrived in the North in the mid-twentieth century, disruption came with hurricane force. In the North we sought to replicate life as we know it in the temperate zone of North America. We believed that Native people in the North should live as we do, and live by our values. We thought of their customs, their values as quaint, perhaps of anthropological interest, but nothing more. And we did not approve of subsistence.

Policy-makers are generally uncomfortable in thinking about the subsistence economy, regarding it as unspecialized, inefficient and unproductive, a "brake on growth." Such economies have not historically generated much surplus, nor have they produced a labour force that is easily adaptable to large-scale industrial enterprise. Hence, policymakers arrived at a moral imperative to bring industrial development to the frontier. The Native way of life based on hunting, fishing and trapping had to go. If it did not, Native people would remain immured in the past.

This resulted not only in the usual bureaucratic muddle, but also in enormous upheaval and colossal mistakes. In the 1950s in the North, Native people were scattered across their traditional territories, living off the land. Deciding this had to be changed, we evacuated them and clustered them in settlements, there to begin a new life.

From Bering Sea to Greenland, European and European-derived

regimes followed these same policies: by Canada in the Yukon Territory and the Northwest Territories, by the United States in Alaska
and by Denmark in Greenland. Public policy proceeded on the assumption that wage and salaried employment could be provided in
these Native villages. This has been the premise accepted by government and industry, and half-adopted by the Native people themselves. They realize now what perhaps they sensed all along: that it
could not be achieved, for throughout the Arctic and sub-Arctic the
state of dependence of Native people, their sense of helplessness, has
increased.

It has always been unwise, indeed it is fraudulent, to claim that for
these villagers wage and salaried employment awaits them. It does
not. To make that statement is not patronizing—it is simply facing
the facts.

We used to think that the changes wrought by science and technology would be altogether benign. In recent years, we have begun
to realize that the advance of science and technology—especially
large-scale technology—may entail social, economic and environmental consequences the costs of which may be enormous. We
understand that all of us may have to pay the costs, but we also understand that in remote frontier regions the burden of such costs
falls disproportionately on Native peoples. The way of the future for
these villagers does not, therefore, lie in large, capital-intensive frontier projects.

So what are the Native people to do? Well, they can do what they
have always done to make a living—they can hunt and fish and trap.
We have always undervalued Native culture, and we have tended to
underestimate the vitality of the Native subsistence economy. We
have, at times, even doubted its existence.

The extent of subsistence hunting and fishing activity in the Arctic and sub-Arctic always comes as a surprise. After the completion
of the Inuit Mapping Project of the 1970s, indicating the scope and
intensity of Native hunting throughout the eastern Arctic, an area as
large as Western Europe, and after the completion of a similar survey in the western Arctic, we in Canada should have known. Yet
there remains a seed of skepticism which sprouts again and again
each time we learn of another survey, anywhere from Alaska to
northern Quebec, which reveals that harvests have not diminished

but have increased. We are surprised once more—yet why should we be? Only because there is no place in our idea of progress for the concept of a viable hunting and fishing economy.

If our specialized vision of progress prevails, it is likely to prevail with indifference to—or even in defiance of—Native aspirations. We have always believed in industrial development and depreciated the indigenous economic base. Indeed, Native people who have tried to earn a living by depending on that base have often been regarded as unemployed.

The failure so far of large-scale industrial projects to provide permanent wage employment for large numbers of Native people has led to expressions of indignation by government officials and by Native people. The real danger of such development, however, is not its failure to provide employment to Native people, but the highly intrusive effect it may have on Native society and especially on the subsistence economy. Industrial development has brought a multiplicity of social problems, problems in the wake of those which had purportedly been solved. Efforts at modernization may have left Native people as mere spectators to their own future.

We are simply not able to provide new economic opportunities to replace the hunting, fishing and trapping economy. The villages of the North must, nevertheless, have an economic base, and in many of them it can only be a subsistence economy based on fish and wildlife resources.

I do not mean to suggest that all Native people can be employed in subsistence activities. Villagers in the Arctic and sub-Arctic continue to depend on employment provided by government activities; even the private sector in these villages is often the product of government expenditures. This is typical of remote villages throughout Arctic and sub-Arctic regions, from Alaska to Greenland. Many Native people want to participate in the opportunities for employment that industrial development offers, and many do. But simply because Native people work alongside workers from the metropolitan centres of North America, it does not mean they have abandoned subsistence. Many Native people have taken advantage of opportunities for wage employment on a limited or seasonal basis to obtain the cash they need to equip or re-equip themselves for subsistence activities. At the end of the day, however, there will not be anything like enough jobs for the Native people in these Northern villages, villages whose populations are still growing.

Native people regard subsistence as their birthright. Wherever I went in the Mackenzie Valley in the 1970s and wherever I went in Alaska in the 1980s, I saw the equipment used for subsistence—snowmobiles, skiffs, nets, sleds, snowshoes, oil drums—and the products of subsistence—racks of drying fish, skins being scraped, smokehouses full of meat. Everywhere the cry was for the defence of subsistence.

In 1975, on the shores of Great Bear Lake, at Fort Franklin, in the Northwest Territories, Chief George Kodakin's fifteen-year-old son Paul showed me on a land use map where he and his father had travelled on hunting trips—the places were the same as those the older people of the village had identified as important traditional hunting grounds. New technology, such as snowmobiles and chartered aircraft, permit the Great Bear Lake Indians to travel quickly to areas far from Fort Franklin, and to spend a shorter time in areas where, in the old days, they would have camped for a whole season. But this has not altered the importance of subsistence activities. Chief Kodakin himself said: "The whole lake is like a deep freeze for Fort Franklin. Our ancestors have used it as a deep freeze and we will use it as a deep freeze for the future children."

Hyacinthe Kochon, the chief at Colville Lake, told me that his people continue to depend upon the land for their livelihood: "Around here we make our living by hunting for our meat, fish on the lakes and trapping. . . . We depend on the land." In Alaska, a decade later, Native people made the same plea in support of the idea of a way of life. At Tenakee, Walter Soboleff, an Aleut elder, explained:

> No matter what the weather may be like, to know that we own land gave us comfort, gave us refuge. It was home. From it we gained food. From it, we gained medicine. On it, we performed the ancient ceremonies. It gave strength to the clan, it gave strength to the family life, and courage and pride to carry on their way of life. And strange as it may seem that, in 1984, that kind of thought still prevails, and it surprises me that the culture is not extinct, like in Egypt or in other parts of the world. It is very much alive.

Dependence on renewable resources continues to define village life. The wage-earning population in most villages is a very small percentage of the whole.

The continuing importance of subsistence was brought home to me in Alaska at Togiak, a Yup'ik village of about six hundred on Bristol Bay. Before I arrived, the school paper announced a potluck supper "to show Judge Berger the variety of subsistence foods." The whole village turned out for the feast, and two high school students escorted me to the head of the line, then to trestle tables laden with food, nearly all of it Native food, with each item labelled—salmon, kelp, walrus, caribou, moose—in all, there were more than twenty Native dishes.

In the *Alaska Native Claims Settlement Act* of 1971 Congress abolished the aboriginal rights of Alaska Natives, including their aboriginal rights of hunting, fishing and trapping. Congress had spoken. Yet twenty years later Alaska Natives refuse to acknowledge the loss of their tribal right, their right as collectivities, to take fish and wildlife and to regulate their own subsistence activities. The Native defence of their right to fish and wildlife resources was best made by a fourteen-year-old Yup'ik boy, Teddy Coopchiak, Jr., at Togiak:

> How should Natives give up their hunting rights? It is well hidden in our mind, and nobody could take it away, like a bird who flies, and nobody could take it or boss it around.
>
> Congress should let the Natives boss themselves, because they have survived during the past. Had to make their own laws then, make their own decisions. That is why they are known to be smart people. That's why they survived in the Arctic for so long.

Today the attack on subsistence comes from a new quarter. Animal rights and animal welfare groups have mounted a series of campaigns against fur harvesting. The principal victims of these campaigns have been the Native people of the Arctic and sub-Arctic regions of North America. These animal rights and animal welfare groups are as ethnocentric as the missionaries, the teachers, the bureaucrats and the representatives of industry. Our European values must be imposed on other people, whether they like it or not. We know best. But this is not just a capricious form of self-indulgence by urbanites seeking another cause; it can cause real damage.

Animal rights and animal welfare groups succeeded in putting an end to the harvest of harp seal pups off the coast of Newfoundland by persuading Europeans that they should not buy any seal fur. Europe is the world's largest market for fashion fur. In 1983, when the European Economic Community boycotted the sale of seal skins, Inuit communities in the North, far removed from the ice floes of Newfoundland where the seal pups are dispatched, found themselves with no market for their furs—furs obtained by the harvesting of mature ringed seals.

The collapse of the market for seal skins has produced hardship in these communities in Canada's eastern Arctic and in Greenland. For many Native people, the sale of fur was their main source of income. Without the money that they earned from pelts, the cash needed to maintain snowmobiles and other gear is unavailable. Hunters may not be able to go out to hunt for food. Many Native people are forced to go on welfare. This sets in motion a sequence of social pathology that may result in tragedy. Anthropologist George Wenzel has said that "In the history of . . . colonial encroachment into the Arctic, there has never been a . . . challenge so directly aimed at the physical and biological base critical to Inuit culture."

The complaints by Native people about campaigns waged by animal rights and animal welfare activists are not confined to the eastern Arctic. In 1985, when I visited the Pribilof Islands off Alaska, I found that the Aleuts there were intensely concerned about the attempt to put an end to the commercial hunting of northern fur seals off the Pribilofs, an attempt that was ultimately successful.

The Aleuts on the Pribilofs, their principal source of income threatened, were unable to comprehend the attitude of the animal rights and animal welfare groups. They can understand it when the oil companies want to drill on Native land and extract oil—they know it is valuable, and they can see the benefit these others seek. But why are people in a far-off metropolis campaigning to prevent them from making a living? What have they got against them? When I was in the Pribilofs the sense of injury and outrage was palpable.

That sense of injury and outrage is shared by other Native peoples in Canada. In 1987, a Cree from northern Quebec, Thomas Coon, speaking of the movement to boycott seal fur, asked:

How would you feel if 60 per cent, 80 per cent, or 90 per cent of your income was taken away from you? How would you feel when you have little children, a family to support? Killing a market is just like taking the food away from the family's table. Those people were poor before the ban, and today they are poorer. . . . Taking life is definitely a cruelty. No matter how we die as human beings, no matter how we take life, it is a cruelty. Killing a culture, killing a society, and killing a way of life is definitely a cruelty. My culture will die in agony.

For some in the animal rights and animal welfare groups theirs is a messianic cause that gives meaning to their own lives. But these activists—largely the offspring of urban, middle-class families—are indulging themselves in a cause the consequences of which they are ignorant. Their thinking is simply another variant on the view, held by many of us, that our values are paramount, that our interests must prevail. The anti-fur lobby is as ignorant of conditions in the North as any representative of government or industry. In 1987, Stephen Best of the International Wildlife Coalition said:

I own about two-thirds of the Native culture. I bought it with my taxes. There would be no Native culture today if . . . Canadians didn't pay for it.

Canada has always subsidized poorer regions of the country. By the same reasoning, Best can claim the right to dictate the way of life of prairie wheat farmers or of the people in Newfoundland's outports, or of all of Canada's old age pensioners.

These bans are not by any means effective in putting an end to the hunting of seals. Although seal pups are no longer taken off Newfoundland, the Inuit still take mature seals, they still regard seal oil as essential to their diet—anyone who, on a cold day in the Arctic, has eaten white fish dipped in seal oil will know the warmth that it brings. They still eat seal meat and wear sealskin clothing in the Arctic winter. So they still take seals. But they cannot sell the fur.

Some of the members of the anti-fur movement think this is right. They believe that Native people should be allowed to hunt wildlife for food, but they should not be allowed to sell the fur. The sacrifice of animals for fur has become the twentieth-century equivalent for the sacrifice of human life attributed to Indians five hundred years ago.

There are also those who believe that subsistence should not include the use of snowmobiles and rifles. Subsistence cultures are not to be allowed to make use of technological advances, to become more efficient in the harvesting of animals. We have so decreed: your values are deficient, your interests are of no consequence, your way of life must remain fixed in amber.

Before contact Native people traded furs among themselves and took advantage of new techniques and new technology developed by their neighbours. The attitude of the anti-fur movement assumes that Native culture is static, that it ought not to be able to change, that Native people should be able to pursue subsistence only in a kind of living folk museum. *Our* values, our interests take precedence. Is this any different from the attitude of the Spaniards who read the Requerimiento to Indians five hundred years ago? Or of the priest who insisted Atahualpa should be converted to Christianity in order to be strangled instead of burned at the stake?

In the late twentieth century many of those in the animal rights and animal welfare movement believe, offhandedly, that the Native people will be better off if they give up subsistence and adopt our way of life. Is this any different from the attitude of the nineteenth-century White people who sympathized with the Indians yet supported the *General Allotment Act,* thinking it would be best for the Indians if they assimilated?

Native people believe in taking animals for fur—fur for their own garments and fur to be sold. But they believe even more fervently in maintaining the great animal populations of the North. They have been in the forefront of the struggle to preserve wilderness and wildlife throughout the North. In the 1970s and 1980s they joined with the environmental movement to protect the Arctic National Wildlife Range in Alaska and to establish the Northern Yukon National Park to safeguard the calving grounds of the Porcupine caribou herd. If Native people had not opposed the construction of a pipeline across the north slope of Alaska and across the northern Yukon we might have lost a herd of 180,000 caribou. To be sure, the failure of the herd to return to its calving grounds would not have been as easy to discern as the dispatching of seal pups, but in the long run it would have caused suffering and losses to animal populations on a scale that can scarcely be comprehended.

The fact is that Native people are not willing to give up subsistence for complete dependence on welfare and wages, founded on the chimera of industrial activity that may not offer assurances for the future and which often stands at cross-purposes to their own cultural imperatives. Industrialism is not only a creator of wealth but also a shatterer of established social systems and a powerful instrument of control in the new social systems to which it gives rise. Its attraction lies not only in the affluence it promises, but also in the freedom it offers from the constraints imposed by nature and tradition. Very few people in the world are inclined to oppose its advance. Native people, however, understand that to embrace it unreservedly will undermine the values they cherish.

With the advance of industry toward the last of our frontiers at a time when the Native peoples' ideas of self-determination are emerging in contemporary forms, the question of the relationship between dominant societies cast in the European mould and Native peoples confronts us again. In the Arctic and sub-Arctic we must consider the question: Are the Native peoples merely a curious cultural backdrop to the activities of European civilization, or are they the peoples for whom the North was made?

Despite our attempts to separate Native people from their language, history and culture, their determination to retain their distinctive identity has sustained them. We see the outward signs of cultural loss and decay; we often do not comprehend the persistence of Native culture and Native values. The Native peoples of the Arctic and sub-Arctic seek to safeguard rights of hunting, fishing and trapping, so as to ensure the survival of subsistence, the principal means by which the Native people in the Arctic and sub-Arctic who still live in villages—as the majority do—can regain a measure of self-sufficiency.

The defence of subsistence can be observed across the North. After Alaska Natives' unhappy experience with the *Alaska Native Claims Settlement Act* of 1971, the Inuit and Indians of James Bay and Northern Quebec insisted, in their 1975 agreement with Canada and Quebec, on measures to strengthen subsistence. So have the Inuit, the Dene and the Metis of Canada's Northwest Territories, and the Indians of the Yukon Territory. In fact, the land claims negotiations of northern Natives, though they deal with sharing revenue from non-renewable resources and a multitude of other matters, are to a great extent concerned with measures to protect and strengthen subsistence. In the same way, the defence of subsistence has driven the movement for restoration of tribal government in Alaska. Native claims are not a retreat into the past but a hard-headed assessment of the present.

We have underestimated the tenacity of Native culture. In the midst of the plethora of social problems they face, Native people are striving for a sense of identity and the means of self-sufficiency in the modern world. They have seen the promise of jobs through industrial development remain unfulfilled. Native people do not oppose industrial development; they believe, however, that they are entitled to a measure of control over the pace of such development and to a share in the wealth that it may create. And they believe that its advent ought not to result in the destruction of the subsistence economy.

Increasingly, in the Arctic and sub-Arctic, Native people are insisting that it is *their* country. They have not been expelled; no one else claims it for living space. In 1975, Gabe Bluecoat of Arctic Red River, speaking to the Mackenzie Valley Pipeline Inquiry, said:

> The land, who made it? I really want to find out who made it. Me? You? The government? Who made it? I know [of] only one man made it—God. But on this land who besides Him made the land? What is given is not sold to anyone. We're that kind of people. What is given to us, we are not going to give away.

In 1984, in Klukwan, a Tlingit village in Alaska, Lonnie Strong said, "Sovereignty derives from the people. Well, we the people are still here."

Native people want distinctly Native interests to be protected. The protection of these interests inevitably means that they seek governmental powers. They want a share in decision-making over land use. They want to be consulted about non-renewable resource development in order to protect renewable resources.

Proposals for Native governments are not a half-way house on the road to assimilation. Native institutions should not be regarded as exceptional or transitional. They are the very means by which Native people can gain a measure of control over their lives.

Countries that have acknowledged individual rights have often opposed the recognition of Native peoples' claims because they imply territorial rights and sovereignty in competition with that of the nation-state. Governments have often opposed the communal holding of land and criticized tribal institutions as neither democratic nor modern. But in the North, what were thought, in the temperate zone, to be compelling reasons for overthrowing Native culture and Native land tenure do not apply. The climate is harsh, the land is not suitable for agriculture, supplies are costly, markets distant. If there is one place in the New World where Native people should have an opportunity to control their land and their future, it is in this brilliant and pitiless landscape.

In 1987, Pope John Paul II came to Fort Simpson, in the Northwest Territories. Addressing Native peoples, he offered this reassurance:

> You are entitled to a just and equitable measure of self-determination, with a just and equitable degree of self-governing. For you a land base with adequate resources is also necessary for developing a viable economy.

Culture must have a material basis. This gives the idea of Native self-determination and the subsistence culture on which it depends a compelling urgency among the peoples of the Arctic and sub-Arctic.

CHAPTER II

Native Claims and the Rule of Law

In 1967 the chiefs of the Nisga'a Tribal Council came to see me at my law office. They wanted to go to court to establish that their Indian title—their aboriginal title—had never been extinguished. The Nisga'a case was to open the way for Native land claims in Canada. This is not to say that in Canada land claims based on aboriginal rights were only recently invented. The Native people had never abandoned their land claims or their claim to aboriginal title; but for a long time such claims were mistaken for the rhetoric of powerlessness.

Canadian ideas about Native peoples have been undergoing a great change. Once thought to be peoples on the margins of the nation's history and irrelevant to present-day concerns, Natives are now seen as having a moral, indeed a constitutional right to fashion a future of their own. Now Canadians realize that aboriginal rights are the axis upon which our relations with the Native peoples turn. This applies as much to the Indians of Canada who have signed treaties as to those with whom treaties were never made, for the treaties themselves were signed to obtain a surrender of aboriginal title. The reserve lands guaranteed by treaty are what remains in Indian ownership of their ancestral lands.

Where Native people are asserting land claims, they do so on the basis of their rights as aboriginal peoples. In the United States and Canada this has given rise to a well-developed theory of aboriginal rights. These rights are unique because at the time of contact aboriginal peoples were present in self-governing, organized political communities, in use and occupation of the land.

Land claims are being advanced by Native peoples all over North and South America. The defence of Native land rights is the issue upon which Native peoples base claims to their identity, culture and political autonomy, and ultimately to their survival. Throughout the New World Native people understand that without a secure land base they will cease to exist as distinct peoples; their fate will be assimilation.

These claims can only be achieved, however, where Native collective identity is acknowledged and their claim to land itself entrenched in the law. Where these are disputed, conflict rages. It is so throughout the New World.

On 28 May 1990, in Ecuador, a thousand Quechua-speaking Indians marched into Quito to present a petition to the nation's president. They chanted "1992 without *haciendas* in Ecuador" and "five hundred years of resistance." They occupied the church of Santo Domingo in downtown Quito. After that, across the Ecuadorean highlands, trees were set alight, roads were blocked and haciendas occupied. The army and the police were ordered to clear the roads. Indians were arrested, but they also took a dozen soldiers hostage. The archbishop of Quito arranged for the hostages to be released, and the occupation of the church ended. The Indians sought the restoration of traditional lands, recognition of Quechua as an official language and compensation for environmental damage to their lands.

In countries such as Ecuador, the suppression of Native rights goes back almost five hundred years, and governments have set their faces against recognition of what they call a nation within a nation. Indian populations in some countries of Latin America comprise anywhere from forty to fifty percent of the population. In Canada, Native numbers are not nearly as large, in absolute terms or as a percentage of the nation's population.

Although Canada did not conduct wars of extermination, Canada's Indian policy went through cycles similar to those in the United States. In Canada the themes of this book have been repeated. In British Columbia we can observe them all: hostility of settlers to Indian rights, decimation of Indians by disease, and only feeble attempts by the central government to protect the Indians.

Ultimately, in Canada, land claims depend on the recognition of the rights of the Indians as aboriginal people. These issues are increasingly being determined by the Supreme Court of Canada in favour of the Indians. In recent years, in British Columbia, and in Canada, decisive changes in policy have been forced upon governments, both federal and provincial, by the courts.

In British Columbia, except for southern Vancouver Island and the Peace River block, no treaties were made with the Indians, and the provincial government's refusal to recognize aboriginal title, coupled with the reluctance of the federal government to insist upon a resolution of the issue, forced the Indians to go to the courts. In British Columbia, Native protest over the loss of their lands has been more audible than elsewhere, and the Indian land question has agitated the province for more than a century. The Nisga'a tribe has been in the forefront of this controversy.

One of the tribes of the northwest coast, the Nisga'a live along the Nass River, which flows into the Pacific at the base of the Alaska Panhandle. Here the sea and the forest have always offered a good life and, before the Europeans arrived, the Indian population along this coast was one of the densest in North America. Here the Nisga'a had their settlements, fishing places and hunting grounds. They regard the Nass River valley as their own.

In Canada, although few treaties were made in the Atlantic provinces and in Quebec, by the mid-eighteenth century the British had established a policy of treating with the Indians for their lands. This policy was enshrined in the Royal Proclamation of 1763. By 1850, treaties had been made with the Indians for the surrender of virtually the whole of southern Ontario; beginning in the 1870s, as settlement proceeded westward across the prairies, treaties were made with the Indians to enable the construction of the Canadian Pacific Railway to proceed, opening the country to settlement. Treaties were also made to allow development of resources on the frontier. The prospect of extracting oil from the Athabasca tar sands, first mooted in the 1880s, led to a treaty in 1899. As late as 1921 a treaty was made with some of the Indian tribes of the Northwest Territories as a consequence of the discovery of oil at Fort Norman.

The British Navy reached the northwest coast of North America late in the eighteenth century when, in 1778, Captain Cook landed at Nootka on Vancouver Island. In 1841, the Hudson's Bay Company established Fort Victoria on Vancouver Island, but settlement began only after 1849, when Vancouver Island was made a Crown colony.

James Douglas, an early governor of the colony, had adopted a policy of treaty-making on Vancouver Island. He thought aboriginal title should be acknowledged, and compensation paid to the Indians. After 1854, Douglas was unable to maintain this policy. The Colonial Office in London would not provide the funds to allow him to do so. The settlers denied that it was their responsibility, and they would not vote funds for the purpose. The colony's House of Assembly had at first acknowledged aboriginal title, but when the House realized that the money for the extinguishment of aboriginal title would have to be provided locally, it began to insist there was no such thing as aboriginal title and no obligation to compensate the Indians for their lands. The mainland colony of British Columbia, established in 1858, also adopted this policy. When the two colonies were united in 1866, the policy continued. In 1867, Joseph Trutch, chief commissioner of lands and works of the newly united colony, wrote:

> The Indians have really no right to the lands they claim, nor are they of any actual value or utility to them, and I cannot see why they should either retain these lands to the prejudice of the general interests of the Colony, or be allowed to make a market of them either to the Government or to Individuals.

Although British Columbia did not recognize aboriginal title, the government of the province did agree that the Indians had to live somewhere, and reserves were set aside for them. The question of aboriginal rights remained outstanding.

In 1871, British Columbia agreed to become a province of Canada. Under the Canadian constitution, jurisdiction over Indians and lands reserved for the Indians is given to the federal government. The dispute over Indian title and Indian reserves became a continuing source of acrimony between Ottawa and British Columbia. The Douglas treaties, made in the 1850s, covered less than one percent of the new province.

In 1872 Trutch, by now lieutenant-governor, wrote to Prime Minister John A. Macdonald:

> If you now commence to buy out Indian title to the lands of B.C. you would go back on all that has been done here for 30 years past and would be equitably bound to compensate the tribes who inhabited the districts now settled [and] farmed by white people equally with those in the more remote and uncultivated portions. . . .

In 1873 Macdonald was thrown out of office as a result of the Pacific Scandal. He was succeeded by a Liberal, Alexander Mackenzie. To the Liberals the claims of the Indians were not a purely academic question. Telesphore Fournier, Mackenzie's minister of justice, raised the question of aboriginal rights in British Columbia in an opinion he wrote recommending disallowance of the province's 1874 *Land Act*. Referring to the policy exemplified by the Royal Proclamation of 1763, he said:

> There is not a shadow of doubt, that from the earliest times, England has always felt it imperative to meet the Indians in council, and to obtain surrenders of tracts of Canada, as from time to time such were required for the purposes of settlement.

But Ottawa was no more successful than Douglas had been in persuading the government of British Columbia to modify its position. Just as Madrid had been unwilling or unable to enforce its will in the New World, just as presidents from George Washington to Ulysses Grant had wrung their hands at the impotence of central authority over frontiersmen determined to take Indian land, so Ottawa did nothing about British Columbia's intransigence.

The Province was a necessary party to any settlement. Under the constitution the province owned all public lands. How could there be a settlement of the land question unless it agreed to contribute land to a settlement? With John A. Macdonald's return to office in 1878, the federal government became less and less willing to intervene in provincial affairs to protect the rights of the Indians.

Examination of the correspondence that passed between Ottawa and British Columbia offers some insight into the nature of federal-provincial conflicts. The Indians themselves, however, do not speak to us through these documents. We know they felt anger and bitter resentment. But what, in fact, was happening to them? How were their lives affected by the progressive loss of their lands and by their confinement to reserves?

When the fur traders arrived, the Indians of the Northwest coast already had a sophisticated culture, one that was at first enriched and refined by contact with the Europeans. Chisels and axes, for instance, made possible great advances in the carving of totem poles. Claude Lévi-Strauss, the French anthropologist, has described the Indian cultures of the northwest coast as one of the remarkable efflorescences of mankind. The collapse of that culture is seen by many as one of the great tragedies of modern times.

Like Indians everywhere in the New World, the Indians of the Northwest coast were defenceless against the diseases brought by the Europeans. Smallpox and tuberculosis took an enormous toll of lives. By 1890, the Indian population of the northwest coast, which at mid-century had stood at about 50,000, was reduced to 10,000, many of whom were enfeebled by disease. The startling decline in the Indian population led to the conclusion, widely held among Whites, that the Indians were a people condemned by history, who would soon become extinct. Any sense of urgency about dealing with the question of aboriginal title diminished year by year.

Nevertheless, in the midst of these calamities, the Indians of the northwest coast continued to cling to their beliefs and to their own idea of themselves. And they remained determined to insist upon their aboriginal rights. In 1887, the provincial government appointed a royal commission "To Enquire into the Conditions of the Indians of the Northwest Coast." When the Commission visited the Nass Valley, the Nisga'a chiefs raised the question of aboriginal rights. David Mackay, one of the chiefs, summed up the Nisga'a point of view:

> What we don't like about the Government is their saying this: "We will give you this much land." How can they give it when it is our own? We cannot understand it. They have never bought it from us or our forefathers. They have never fought and conquered our people and taken the land in that way, and yet they say now that they will give us so much land—our own land. [Our] chiefs do not talk foolishly, they know the land is their own; our forefathers for generations and generations past had their land here all around us; chiefs have had their own hunting grounds, their salmon streams, and places where they got their berries; it has always been so. . . . it has been ours for thousands of years.

Nevertheless, pressure on Indian lands continued. In 1885 the completion of the Canadian Pacific Railway had brought a rush of new immigrants. British Columbia, which had been easily accessible only by the Pacific, could now be reached by rail from eastern Canada. By the end of the century, the province's White population had greatly increased, and the resource industries and the road and rail networks had been extended throughout most of the province.

The Indians still had their reserves, of course. Encroachment on these lands followed the same pattern as in the United States and Chile, though not with the same violence. After the turn of the century the province refused to lay out any more reserves. It insisted, instead, that the existing reserves must be reduced in size and that lands already held by the Indians must be made available for agricultural and commercial uses.

All this time, the Indians continued to press for recognition of their aboriginal title. The province, however, would not change its position. In 1909, the premier of British Columbia, Richard McBride, said "Of course it would be madness to think of conceding to the Indians' demands. It is too late to discuss the equity of dispossessing the Red man in America." McBride believed that the question of aboriginal title would never have been raised were it not for the "pernicious advice of some unscrupulous Whites." This idea recurs again and again in our dealings with the Native peoples. Many Whites have always found it convenient to believe that Native people would not have thought of asserting their claims to the land, if it were not for the influence of subversive Whites.

When Premier McBride continued to demand reductions in the size of reserves in the province, the two governments agreed to establish a joint royal commission to make a final and complete "adjustment" of Indian lands in British Columbia. From 1912 to 1916, the McKenna-McBride Commission travelled throughout the province to take evidence. In 1915, its members visited the Nass Valley, where Gideon Minesque spoke for the Nisga'a:

> We haven't got any ill feelings in our hearts but we are just waiting for this thing to be settled and we have been waiting for the last five years—it is not only a short time that we have lived here; we have been living here from time immemorial—it has been handed down in legends from the old people and that is what hurts us very much because the White people have come along and taken this land away from us. . . . We have heard that some white men . . . said that the [Nisga'as] must be dreaming when they say they own the land upon which they live. It is not a dream—we are certain that this land belongs to us. Right up to this day the government never made any treaty, not even to our grandfathers or our great-grandfathers.

To Gideon Minesque, the facts were plain enough. The Nisga'a were the original inhabitants of the valley. They had lived there from time immemorial. They had no doubt that the land belonged to them: "It is not a dream—we are certain. . . . " Gideon Minesque was addressing the question of Indian title. The Commission, however, restricted itself to the allotment of land for reserves. In British Columbia as a whole the Commission confirmed some of the existing reserves, and it added about 35,000 hectares of new reserve land. But the Commission removed from the reserves some 20,000 hectares of land the Indians held. These "cut-off" lands were far more valuable than the lands given to the Indians to replace them. What the Commission had done was to remove from the reserves good land that Whites wanted and to replace it with poor land.

The Nisga'a and other tribes continued to raise the issue of aboriginal title. They were treated, by both levels of government, not as a people with a claim deserving of fair and honourable consideration, but as mendicants. Aboriginal title was officially regarded as belonging to a world of the past. Determined that this question should never be raised again, the Parliament of Canada included a provision in the *Indian Act* of 1927 that made it an offence punishable by law to raise funds for the purpose of pursuing any Indian land claim. It was not until 1951 that this prohibition was repealed.

Although the Indian land question was no longer a public issue, the Indian people did not regard the issue as closed. In 1967, the Nisga'a Indians filed a lawsuit in the Supreme Court of British Columbia. Their claim was a simple one. Indian title, they alleged, had never been extinguished in British Columbia. In their suit brought against the Province, the Nisga'a asked the court for a declaration that their aboriginal title had never been lawfully extinguished. In April 1969, the trial of the Nisga'a Indians' claim opened in the Supreme Court of British Columbia.

The Province argued that aboriginal title was a concept unknown to the law and that, even if such title had existed, it had been extinguished by the old Colony of British Columbia before it became a province of Canada in 1871. Of course, since the Constitution conferred exclusive jurisdiction over Indian lands on the federal government, once British Columbia had entered Confederation only the federal government could extinguish Indian title. It was conceded that the federal government had not taken any action since Confederation to extinguish aboriginal title in British Columbia.

The evidence of Professor Wilson Duff, an anthropologist from the University of British Columbia and the leading scholar in the province on northwest coast Indian ideas of aboriginal title, described the concept of Indian title as understood by the Indians themselves. A passage from his book *The Indian History of British Columbia* was read into the record to demonstrate the point.

> It is not correct to say that the Indians did not own land but only roamed over the face of it and used it. The patterns of

ownership and utilization which they imposed upon the lands and waters were different from those recognized by our system of law, but were nonetheless clearly defined and mutually respected. Even if they didn't subdivide and cultivate the land, they did recognize ownership of plots used for village sites, fishing places, berry and root patches, and similar purposes. Even if they didn't subject the forests to wholesale logging, they did establish ownership of tracts used for hunting, trapping, and food gathering. Even if they didn't sink mine shafts into the mountains, they did own peaks and valleys for mountain goat hunting and as sources of raw materials. Except for barren and inaccessible areas which are not utilized even today, every part of the province was formerly within the owned and recognized territory of one or other of the Indian tribes.

The case for the Province rested on a series of statutes passed by the Colony of Vancouver Island and the Colony of British Columbia, which enabled the Crown to make grants of land to the settlers. But these statutes made no mention of aboriginal title; certainly they did not purport to abolish aboriginal title. The contention of the Province was that this exercise of legislative power had operated to extinguish whatever interest the Indians may have had in the lands comprising British Columbia, albeit without compensation. After all, how could it be said that Indian title still existed when the pre-Confederation governments had assumed the power to dispose of the very lands the Indians claimed? By disregarding aboriginal title, argued the Province, the Crown had extinguished it.

The trial judge accepted this argument and dismissed the Nisga'a claim. He held that, if aboriginal title had existed, it had been extinguished by the statutes passed by the old colonial governments of Vancouver Island and British Columbia.

The Nisga'a carried their case to the British Columbia Court of Appeal. There they suffered another setback. The trial judge had not determined whether or not there is such a thing as aboriginal title; he had simply held that, if there were such a title, it had been extinguished before the colony entered Confederation. He left to higher courts the determination of whether or not aboriginal title was a concept recognized by Canadian law. The British Columbia Court of Appeal was ready to address the question. The judges of that court

held that the law had never acknowledged any such concept as aboriginal title, that although governments might choose as a matter of
policy to deal with Indians as if they did have a legal interest in land,
there was, in reality, no such legal interest—no Indian title—there
never had been. Thus the Nisga'a had never had aboriginal title to
the Nass Valley. The Court of Appeal went on to say that, even if
they had had such a title, it had been extinguished during the pre-
Confederation era. Chief Justice H.W. Davey demonstrated the attitude of the court, one of ancient lineage. In 1550 Sepúlveda had
argued, "They do not even have private property." Observing the
Nisga'a across an ethnographic gulf, Chief Justice Davey declined to
believe that the Nisga'a had their own ideas of land ownership, saying, "They were undoubtedly at the time of settlement a very primitive people with few institutions of civilized society, and none at all
of our notions of private property."

It was difficult to convince lawyers and judges that the Native
peoples of Canada possess rights based on the indisputable fact that
they occupied vast areas if not the whole of this continent before the
Europeans colonized it. They had their own institutions, their own
laws. But of this lawyers and judges remained unaware. They could
not accept that people without a written language can, nevertheless,
have an elaborate legal system of their own. And, as for their aboriginal title, how could the court acknowledge it? It was ill defined, it
was not recorded in a system of title deeds and land registration; it
was not a form of private property but property held communally by
the tribe or clan.

Chief Justice Davey's inability to comprehend the true nature of
Native culture and Native claims is widely shared. It results in an attitude toward Native people that exasperates them when it does not
infuriate them. This attitude is sometimes manifested in an attempt
to preserve Native culture and sometimes in an attempt to eradicate
it, but it is always manifested in a patronizing way. It assumes that
Native culture cannot be viable in a contemporary context. This is
the crux of the matter. Native peoples insist that their culture is still
a vital force in their own lives, that it informs their own view of
themselves, of the world about them, and of the dominant society.
We too easily assume that Native culture is moribund.

Prime Minister Pierre Trudeau, speaking on the subject of aboriginal rights in Vancouver on 8 August 1969, said, "Our answer is no.

We can't recognize aboriginal rights because no society can be built on historical 'might have beens'." So there was no relief to be had in the courts, and no acknowledgement of Indian claims by the federal government. But the Native peoples' belief that their past has a place in their future, that the rights they enjoyed before contact were not a chimera, led the Nisga'a to appeal to the Supreme Court of Canada. This appeal was to be one of the principal instruments of the overthrow of Canadian government policy.

But wasn't Trudeau right? Shouldn't Native peoples be treated as any other minority? Why should there be a special place for them in the constitution and in the life of the nation? No such provision was made for the Ukrainians, the Swedes, the Italians, or for any other ethnic group or nationality. The distinction is that the Native people did not immigrate to Canada as individuals or families who expected to be assimilated. Immigrants chose to come to Canada and to submit to the nation's laws and institutions; their choices were individual choices. The Native peoples, however, were already here: they have been forced to submit to the laws and institutions of the dominant White society. They have never relinquished their claim to be treated as distinct peoples in our midst.

The chiefs of the Nisga'a villages in the Nass Valley, together with village elders wearing their traditional sashes, travelled to Ottawa for the hearing in November 1971. Seven judges of the Supreme Court of Canada sat on the case. The argument of the appeal took five days. The judges reserved their decision for fourteen months. In February 1973 when the Court handed down its judgement, the Nisga'as appeared to have lost, four to three. They had reached the end of the road. But careful study of the reasoning of the seven judges who heard the case soon made it clear that, although technically the Nisga'a had lost their case, they had in fact won a moral victory. Moral victories are not usually of any tangible value, but this victory brought about a fundamental change in federal government policy.

Mr. Justice Wilfred Judson, writing for three judges, found that the Nisga'a, before the coming of the Europeans, had aboriginal title, a title recognized under English law. But, he went on to say, this title had been extinguished by the old Colony of Vancouver Island and the Colony of British Columbia. Mr. Justice Emmett Hall, writing for three other judges, found that the Nisga'a, before the coming of the Europeans, had aboriginal title, that it had never been extinguished, and that this title could be asserted even today. On this reckoning the court was tied.

All of the six judges who had addressed the main question supported the view that English law in force in British Columbia when colonization began had recognized Indian title to the land. The seventh judge held against the Nisga'a on a technicality. Nevertheless, for the first time, Canada's highest court had unequivocally affirmed the concept of aboriginal title. Mr. Justice Judson, in describing the nature of Indian title, concluded:

> The fact is that when the settlers came the Indians were there, organized in societies and occupying the land as their forefathers had done for centuries. This is what Indian title means. . . . What they are asserting in this action is that they had a right to continue to live on their lands as their forefathers had lived and that this right has never been lawfully extinguished.

Mr. Justice Judson went on to hold that the pre-Confederation enactments of the old colonies had effectively extinguished the aboriginal title of the Nisga'a Indians, before British Columbia entered Confederation, but he had no doubt that aboriginal title had always been recognized under the common law.

Mr. Justice Hall, writing for the three judges who were prepared to uphold the Nisga'a claim, urged that the courts should adopt a contemporary view and not be bound by past and mistaken notions about Indians and Indian culture. In the judgement of Mr. Justice Hall you will find that sense of humanity—that stretch of the mind and heart—that enabled him to look at the idea of aboriginal rights and to see it as the Indian people see it. This required an understanding of the place of Indian history in Canadian history. He suggested that Chief Justice Davey, in asserting that the [Nisga'a] were at the time of settlement "a very primitive people with few of the institutions of civilized society, and none at all of our notions of private property," had assessed Indian culture by the same standards that the Europeans applied to the Indians of North America two or more centuries before. Mr. Justice Hall rejected this approach. He said:

The assessment and interpretation of the historical documents and enactments tendered in evidence must be approached in the light of present-day research and knowledge disregarding ancient concepts formulated when understanding of the customs and culture of our original people was rudimentary and incomplete and when they were thought to be wholly without cohesion, laws or culture, in effect a subhuman species. This concept of the original inhabitants of America led Chief Justice Marshall in his otherwise enlightened judgement in *Johnson v. McIntosh* . . . to say: "But the tribes of Indians inhabiting this country were fierce savages whose occupation was war. . . . " We know now that this assessment was ill-founded. The Indians did in fact at times engage in some tribal wars but war was not their vocation and it can be said that their preoccupation with war pales into insignificance when compared to the religious and dynastic wars of "civilized" Europe of the 16th and 17th centuries.

Mr. Justice Hall concluded that the Nisga'a had their own concept of aboriginal title before the coming of the Europeans and were entitled to assert it today. He said:

What emerges from the . . . evidence is that the [Nisga'a] in fact are and were from time immemorial a distinctive cultural entity with concepts of ownership indigenous to their culture and capable of articulation under the common law. . . .

Emmett Hall's contributions to Canadian life are numerous. None is more important than his judgement in the Nisga'a case, for he held that the Nisga'a title could be asserted today. He ruled that unless legislation evinced a clear and plain intention to extinguish Indian title, it could not be said to have been extinguished.

The decision catapulted the question of aboriginal title into the political arena. On 8 August 1973, the federal government announced that it intended to settle native land claims in all parts of Canada where no treaties had yet been made. Mr. Justice Hall's judgement had become the basis for the assertion of Native land claims throughout Canada.

Canada's new Constitution, adopted 19 April 1982, contains a guarantee of Native rights: "The existing aboriginal rights and treaty rights of the aboriginal peoples of Canada are hereby recognized and affirmed." These words are binding not only on the federal government but also on the provinces. They give the Native people the means to enforce their right to a distinct place in the life of the nation.

Thus far the signs are encouraging. On 31 May 1990, in a case called *R. v. Sparrow,* the Supreme Court of Canada handed down a unanimous judgement, seventeen years after the split decision in the Nisga'a case, breaking the tie. It upheld the judgement of Mr. Justice Hall. The case involved aboriginal fishing rights in British Columbia; the Court had to determine whether aboriginal fishing rights had been extinguished. Chief Justice Brian Dickson and Mr. Justice Gerald La Forest, writing for the court, said: "The test of extinguishment to be adopted, in our opinion, is that the Sovereign's intention must be clear and plain if it is to extinguish an aboriginal right." They held that the aboriginal fishing right in the case before them had not been extinguished.

The Court, in its reasons for judgement, recited the long history of injustice towards Canada's Indians, stating "We cannot recount with much pride the treatment accorded to the Native people of this Country." Why this *mea culpa?* It is not guilt. None of us were there when the land was taken. Rather it is a visceral acknowledgement that as far as the Indians are concerned, *this was their country,* and it was taken from them. Hence the Court's implied message that there must be a political settlement. Finally, in March 1991, the Province of British Columbia agreed to become a party to land claims negotiations.

Settlement of their claims ought to offer the Native peoples a whole range of opportunities. In some cases priority should be given to local renewable resource activities—not because such activities are universally desirable, but because they are on a scale appropriate to many Native communities. These are activities that local people can undertake, that are amenable to local management and control, and that are related to traditional values. There is no reason, however, why Native peoples should not have access as well to the economy of the dominant society where large-scale technology predominates. The settlement of Native claims ought to provide the means to enable Native peoples to thrive, and Native cultures to develop, in ways denied them in the past. They can become hunters, trappers, fishermen, lawyers, loggers, doctors, nurses, teachers, workers in the oil and gas fields, or in the sawmills and the stores. But most important of all, the collective fabric of Native life must be affirmed and strengthened. The sense of identity of individual Native people—their very well-being—depends upon it.

Native people do not want to recreate a world that has vanished. They do, however, want to find a secure place in the world that we have forced upon them. Indian treaties, Indian reserves, Indian Acts—these are all institutions that Europeans have devised to manage Native people primarily for the convenience of the dominant society. Now, Native people want to develop institutions of their own fashioning; they are eager to see their cultures grow and change in directions they have chosen for themselves. They do not wish to be objects of sentimentality. They do not want to return to life in tipis and igloos. They are citizens of the twentieth century. However, just because Native people use the technology of the dominant society, that fact does not mean that they should learn no history except that of the dominant society, or that they should be governed by European institutions alone.

If, in working out settlements of Native claims, we try to force Native development into moulds that we have cast, the whole process will end in failure. No tidy, bureaucratic chart will be of any use: no governmental policy or programme can succeed unless it takes into account Native peoples' determination to remain themselves.

Will the politicians seek to limit the scope of any settlement so as to leave unanswered the very question of the structure of relations between the dominant society and the Native peoples—the question that will await us no matter how long we seek to avoid it?

When the Europeans came, the Indians were already here, with their own institutions and ways of life. They are not fragments of some civilization overseas, consisting of individuals or family groups that made their way to the New World. For them there is no "old country" which will perpetuate their culture if they do not.

The proposals that Native people are making are, many of them, far-reaching. They should not, however, be regarded as a threat to established institutions, but as an opportunity to affirm our commitment to the human rights of aboriginal peoples. We must not make the mistake of underestimating the commitment that men and women have to those who share their own identity and their own past. The commitment they share is more powerful than any ideology.

Epilogue

L as Casas called upon Spain to consider by what right one race imposes its laws and institutions upon another. Today, we are still struggling with the implications of that question, though it does not arise in precisely the same terms as it did at the threshold of European occupation of the Native domain. Nevertheless, we ask ourselves: by what measures can we establish a fair and equitable relationship between dominant societies, cast in the European mould, and the Native peoples?

There are perhaps fifty million Native people in North and South America, almost everywhere dispossessed, poor and powerless. In the past they refused to die; today they will not be assimilated. They insist that we must address the issues that have pursued us since Columbus made his landfall in the West Indies.

The people of the industrialized nations think of the city, of the metropolis, as the mirror of progress. The history of the New World is the history of the frontier, of pushing back the wilderness, cultivating the soil, populating the land and building an industrial way of life. The conquest of North and South America is a unique episode in human history; it altered the face of two continents. With it a particular idea of progress became fixed in our consciousness.

Claude Lévi-Strauss notes, in *Tristes Tropiques,* when discussing "the confrontation between the Old World and the New":

> Enthusiastic partisans of the idea of progress are in danger of failing to recognize—because they set so little store by them— the immense riches accumulated by the human race on either side of the narrow furrow on which they keep their eyes fixed; by under-rating the achievements of the past, they devalue all those which still remain to be accomplished.

Often, therefore, our attitude towards Native cultures has been a patronizing one. It has too often led us to dismiss Native societies as poor and acutely disadvantaged anachronisms in a modern world. After all, the Iroquois today are embroiled in internecine disputes; the Nisga'a still await the settlement of their claims; the descendants of the Maya are defenceless in their tribal homeland; the Mapuche land is now irretrievably lost; the Indians of Amazonia await the dissolution of their tribal ties.

Would the Native people be better off if they assimilated? It might seem better for us; we would not be confronted daily with the racial embodiment of a grievance that will not go away. If the Native people were to assimilate, however, each of our countries would lose an element of diversity. If the Native people's relationship to the environment is one we should emulate, it would be there no longer for us to study.

At bottom, however, it is a question of human rights. Political theories designed for Europe will not be complete in the New World until they provide a place for the rights of Native collectivities. This is the point: in 1550 Las Casas said, "All the peoples of the world are men." In 1987 Pope John Paul II said, speaking to Canada's Native peoples at Fort Simpson, "You are entitled to take your rightful place among the peoples of the earth."

Assumption No

Today, if we chanced upon a land hitherto unknown, inhabited by a people with their own laws and institutions, we would not assume the right to appropriate their land and subjugate them. If we are to have a world based on the rule of law, the nations of Europe and their successors that displaced the Native peoples of the New World must recognize that the precepts of international law now require a fair accommodation with the Native peoples.

The clock cannot be turned back, and the rule of discovery vitiated retroactively. Under international law, the rule of effective occupation stands in the way. But a measure of self-rule could be accorded to Native people within the constitutional set-up of the nation-states of North and South America.

Our ideas of the nation-state, of what government looks like, were developed in Europe. In the New World the nation-state became firmly entrenched. Native peoples have been almost suffocated by the insistence that they subscribe to our ideologies, whether nationalist, democratic, capitalist or Marxist. There has been no room for competing loyalties.

But why should the political institutions, the machinery of government, have been established here in the New World on precisely the same lines as in Europe, and in ways calculated to oppress and impoverish the indigenous inhabitants? Native peoples believe that their future lies in the assertion of their own common identity and the defence of their own common interests. To do this, they must enjoy institutions of self-government that enable them to defend their land. This is what, for Native peoples, land claims and sovereignty are all about.

Why have we been unwilling to countenance such arrangements? Why should the idea of political and economic progress not be broad enough to encompass the future of the Native peoples as distinct societies, distinct political communities, in our midst?

Their loyalty is to the family, the kinship group, the tribe, to their first nations—a loyalty that comes before their loyalty to the nation-state. An anomaly? Why? Why should we think of the nation-state as the highest stage of political development, that a citizen must, in deference to the nation-state, shed all other loyalties?

This is not to say that every country has been resistant to change. In recent years Native people in both North and South America have made themselves heard; they have measurably advanced their cause.

In the 1970s the Supreme Court of the United States fleshed out the meaning of Indian sovereignty. In 1982 Canada amended its Constitution to recognize and affirm existing aboriginal and treaty rights. In Latin America changes can be discerned: Brazil's new Constitution, adopted in 1988, offers a measure of recognition to Indian rights. Colombia has begun to move towards recognition of Indian land rights and Indian self-government. In Argentina a new statute recognizes certain rights in Argentina's surviving Indian populations.

But none of these measures will result in changes in the lives of Native people unless they reflect alterations in our attitudes towards Native people as well as alterations in our legal relations with them. These measures are not the end, they are merely the beginning, the beginning of an attempt to redress five hundred years of history. We must be willing therefore to re-examine the architecture of the nation-state, even to knock out a few walls. This will mean truly innovative political arrangements.

Neither the Native people today, nor their ancestors, should be romanticized. Whether by sentimentalizing them or anathematizing them—both are means of thinking of them as the 'other,' as alien. Make no mistake, they are people of our own time. They are like ourselves—flawed, full of paradoxes, infuriating in their variety. At the end of the day, however, they are human beings: this was their country; they survive as collectivities among us.

The culture of Native people amounts to more than crafts and carvings. Their tradition of decision-making by consensus, their respect for the wisdom of their elders, their concept of the extended family, their belief in a special relationship with the land, their regard for the environment, their willingness to share—all of these values persist in one form or another within their own culture, even though they have been under unremitting pressure to abandon them.

Land claims and self-government are not ancient, forgotten and specious, but current and contemporary. They are, for Native peoples, the means to the preservation of their culture, their languages, and where possible their economic mode—the means by which they can continue to assert their distinct identity and still have access to the social, economic and political institutions of the dominant society.

Of course, some will object, these ambitions are racist. How can a liberal democracy tolerate political institutions limited to persons of one race? To Native people, this objection seems mindless. They were here first. This is not just a trite saying; it is the basis of their case. They were here, governing themselves; theirs was the only race inhabiting the continent. After the Europeans came and occupied the continent, driving the Natives into enclaves, even these enclaves came under attack, because they were limited to Native people. But they are political communities, founded on tradition and culture, not on race. These communities are not vestigial: rather they are the repositories of Native hopes and ideals of self-government.

Notwithstanding a series of apocalyptic predictions, Native societies have persisted for five hundred years. We expect that they will persist for another five hundred years and beyond. Do they not deserve a chance on their own terms? Native peoples *will* not be assimilated, and their fierce wish to retain their own culture is intensifying as industry, technology and communications forge a larger and larger mass culture, extruding diversity.

I believe, too, that it is essential to remember those who suffered and died; the millions of Native victims of violence, cruelty and disease. Each of the Native peoples has had to pass through an inferno. We owe it to our belief in our own humanity—and theirs—to ensure they are not forgotten.

There are no easy solutions. But we should insist that, in our relations with the Native people, we live by our own beliefs. There must be a commitment to human rights, a determination to erode, inch by inch, the conditions which have made Native people strangers in their own land. They must have the means to maintain their identity, to thrive and to prosper.

Practical voices will say it is out of the question, that their only future lies in assimilation. But unless assimilation occurs by enforced social engineering on a Stalinist scale, there will be no assimilation. The Native people have survived draconian measures for half a millennium. They may be poor, they may be oppressed, but they know who they are.

Pablo Neruda described Macchu Picchu as "High reef of the human dawn." From that high place we can trace the signs of the Native peoples' journey across time and the continents. Their journey is not over; our journey together has yet to begin.

In 1992, we will celebrate the triumph of Europe in North and

South America. Nevertheless, almost anywhere you look on the map, the original inhabitants remain; they have survived wars of extermination, the ravages of disease, marginalization and unceasing attempts to assimilate them; they have fought tenaciously to maintain their identity, their culture and the remnants of their land. This is equally a triumph, a triumph of the human spirit, as much to be celebrated as the success of the European enterprise.

This is still the age of discovery, a discovery of the true meaning of the history of the New World and of the Native peoples' rightful place in that world. This is a discovery to be made in our own time, should we choose it—the second discovery of America.

Chapter Notes

I have drawn upon my experience as a lawyer for Native people. I have also drawn upon my experience in the North, which has taken me to Native villages from Bering Sea to Hudson Bay. I have been to many Native communities throughout Canada and the United States.

I cannot pretend to know the countries south of the Rio Grande. I have travelled to Mexico, the Caribbean, and South America. No one could expect to visit all these countries and, even in a lifetime, to get to know them intimately. All I can say is that I have read much of the work of Eduardo Galeano and Gabriel García Márquez. Nor could any one in a lifetime master the literature covering five hundred years of White-Native relations in two continents. I have depended on Drew Ann Wake, who researched material for chapters dealing with South America, and whose long experience in South America and knowledge of the literature was especially helpful to me.

I have relied as well on my reading, my informants, and my own impressions in my travels. In these chapter notes I wish to pay tribute to the authors whom I have particularly relied upon.

A few comments on usage. As the first inhabitants of the New World the Spanish encountered were called by them "Indians," I have used the phrase "Indians" exclusively early in the book to describe the peoples of the New World. I use the expression "Native people" where it seems appropriate. As Chapter 10 brings the book to the Arctic and sub-Arctic, where, besides Indians, there are Eskimos (a word the Inupiat and Yup'ik of Alaska use to describe themselves generically) and Aleuts, and, in northern Canada, besides Indians, the Inuit and the Métis, I have used these words where called for. Many Native persons today refer to their collectivities as First Nations. No doubt this is appropriate for them. In a historical discussion, it is better, I think, to refer to the expressions used and understood at the time. I have referred to African slaves as such, and later to Black slaves, for the same reason.

I have used the spellings for the Yup'ik and Inupiat people of Alaska and for the Inuvialuit of Canada's western Arctic that I used in *Village Journey: Report of the Alaska Native Review Commission* (New York: Hill & Wang, 1985) and in *Northern Frontier, Northern Homeland: Report of the Mackenzie Valley Pipeline Inquiry* (Ottawa, Department of Supply and Services, Canada, 1977).

I have referred to Whites, an expression which, like Europeans, includes persons of all races who have assimilated to the dominant European-derived societies of North and South America. I have chosen to refer to Europe rather than to the West. I have referred to England and the English in discussing events which occurred in the years before the union of England and Scotland in 1707; after that to Great Britain and to the British.

Where I have referred to works written in Spanish and which have not been translated into English, I have relied on Drew Ann Wake's translation. The title of this book was suggested by a phrase from Hugh Brody's recent book, *The People's Land* (Vancouver: Douglas & McIntyre, 1991).

INTRODUCTION

J. E. Chamberlin has been here before. See his insightful discussion of White-Native relations in North America from the earliest times, *The Harrowing of Eden: White Attitudes toward Native Americans* (New York: Seabury Press, 1975).

The quotation from Pablo Neruda, translated by Nathaniel Tarn, is from *The Heights of Macchu Picchu* (New York: The Noonday Press; Farrar, Straus & Giroux, 1966).

CHAPTER 1:
LAS CASAS AND THE RIGHTS OF THE INDIANS

I have made Las Casas the main protagonist of the Indian cause. I am aware, however, that in 1511 Father Antonio Montesinos, another Dominican, preceded Las Casas in denouncing Spanish cruelty, in a sermon at the cathedral in Santo Domingo.

Las Casas's most famous work is his *History of the Indies,* translated and edited by Andrée M. Collard (New York: Harper Torchbooks, 1971). Lewis Hanke's works, especially *Aristotle and the American Indians* (Chicago: Henry Regnery Company, 1959), reveal the continuing influence of Las Casas. See also Juan Friede and Benjamin Keene, *Bartolomé de Las Casas in History: Toward an Understanding of the Man and His Work* (Dekalb: Northern Illinois University Press, 1971); Wagner and Parish, *The Life and Writings of Bartolomé de Las Casas* (Albuquerque: University of New Mexico Press, 1967).

The two accounts given by the Dominicans of Spanish savagery in the Caribbean are found in Tzvetan Todorov, translated by Richard Howard, *The Conquest of America* (New York: Harper & Row, 1984).

Everyone who writes about the conquest of the Aztecs relies on the account of Cortés's expedition by Bernal Díaz, *The Conquest of New Spain,* translated by J. M. Cohen (Harmondsworth: Penguin Books, 1963). W. H. Prescott's *The Fall of the Spanish Empire* includes the *Conquest of the Aztecs,* which appeared in 1843, and the *Conquest of Peru,* which appeared in 1847. John Hemming's *The Conquest of the Incas* (London: Macmillan, 1970) is the most complete modern account. It is immensely useful, in fact indispensable. Alfred Métraux, translated from the French by George Ordish, *The History of the Inca Empire* (New York: Random House, 1969) is also excellent.

Las Casas did not at first have the same attitude toward Indians and Blacks: he agreed that the latter, but not the former, should be reduced to slavery. But enslavement of Blacks was already established in Las Casas's time, whereas that of the Indians had only begun. When Las Casas wrote the *History of the Indies*, he said that he no longer made any distinction between the two groups.

CHAPTER 2: THE DEBATE AT VALLADOLID

I have not mentioned Francisco de Vitoria, who had earlier written on the rights of the Indians, arguing that they should not be enslaved. His work was the basis for much of the debate at Valladolid. He was not always consistent, however, with regard to such subjects as a just war and its relationship to Indian slavery.

Lewis Hanke has written an account of the debate at Valladolid: *All Mankind is One: A Study of the Disputation Between Bartolomé de Las Casas and Juan Ginés de Sepúlveda on the Religious and Intellectual Capacity of the American Indians* (Dekalb: Northern Illinois University Press, 1974).

All of the themes of this chapter relating to European attitudes about the Indians, including the significance to Europeans of human sacrifice and the eating of human flesh by Indians are developed in Anthony Pagden, *The Fall of Natural Man: The American Indian and the Origins of Comparative Ethnology* (Cambridge: Cambridge University Press, 1982).

CHAPTER 3: DISEASE AND DEATH

The statistics regarding Indian demographic losses are discussed in *Cambridge History of Latin America,* ed. Leslie Bethell, Vol. III (Cambridge: Cambridge University Press, 1984). See also Charles Gibson, *The Aztecs under Spanish Rule: A History of the Indians of the Valley of Mexico, 1519–1810* (Stanford: Stanford University Press, 1964).

William H. McNeill, *Plagues and Peoples* (Garden City, New York: Anchor Press Doubleday, 1976), suggests that disease played a great part in the conquests by the Spaniards, militarily and culturally.

Darcy Ribeiro's study originally appeared under the title, "Culturas e Linguas Indígenas do Brasil," in *Educação e Ciencias Sociais* (Rio de Janeiro, 1957); it is translated and reprinted in Janice H.

Hopper, ed., *Indians of Brazil in the Twentieth Century* (Washington, D. C., 1967). Ribeiro's work and the recent history of the Indians of Brazil is discussed by Shelton H. Davis, *Victims of the Miracle: Development and the Indians of Brazil* (Cambridge and New York: Cambridge University Press, 1977).

The quotation "Great was the stench . . . ", is found in *Plagues and Peoples,* supra, at p. 216, and is taken from the *Annals of the Cakchiquels and Title of the Lords of Totonicapan,* Adrian Recinos, et al., trans. (Norman: University of Oklahoma Press, 1953).

Bruce Trigger, in *Natives and Newcomers: Canada's "Heroic Age" Reconsidered* (Montreal and Kingston: McGill-Queen's University Press, 1985) has suggested that, once smallpox was established in the West Indies, Spanish, French or English ships brought it to the North American mainland (p. 236). Trigger, in the same work, has summarized the literature on the pre-contact Native population of North America north of the Rio Grande, reviewing the work of Alfred L. Kroeber, Henry F. Dobyns and Ann F. Ramenofsky. And see especially Ann F. Ramenofsky, *Vectors of Death: The Archeology of European Contact* (Albuquerque: University of New Mexico Press, 1987).

I have also relied on my own study *Northern Frontier, Northern Homeland: Report of the Mackenzie Valley Pipeline Inquiry* (Ottawa: Queen's Printer, 1977; rev. ed., Douglas & McIntyre, 1988), and on my *Report of Advisory Commission on Indian and Inuit Health Consultation* (Ottawa: Department of Supply and Services, 1980).

I have referred to the Eskimos as Eskimos until the discussion reaches our own time, when I use the contemporary usages, such as Inuit. So I have referred to the Mackenzie Eskimos as Eskimos because that is how they were known at the turn of the century. The contemporary Canadian usage, applicable to all peoples who used to be called Eskimos, is Inuit, and I use this latter expression in relating events in our own time. The Inuit in fact include a number of peoples, the Inuvialuit being the descendants of the Mackenzie Eskimos.

CHAPTER 4: INDIAN SLAVERY:
BRAZIL AND THE CAROLINAS

No one can write about the Indians of Brazil without paying tribute to John Hemming's works, *Red Gold: The Conquest of the Brazilian Indians* (Cambridge: Harvard University Press, 1978) and *Amazon Fron-*

tier: The Defeat of the Brazilian Indians (Cambridge: Harvard University Press, 1987). E. Bradford Burns, *A History of Brazil,* 2d ed. (New York: Columbia University Press, 1980) provides a very good overview.

Gary B. Nash's *Red, White, and Black: The Peoples of Early America,* 2d ed. (Englewood Cliffs: Prentice-Hall, 1982) is excellent, offering a complete account of the development of the slave trade in the Carolinas. I have also relied on D. W. Meinig, *The Shaping of America: A Geographical Perspective on 500 Years of History,* Vol. 1, *Atlantic America, 1492–1800* (New Haven: Yale University Press, 1986).

Wesley Frank Craven, in *White, Red, and Black: The Seventeenth Century Virginian* (Charlottesville: The University Press of Virginia, 1971), discussed the beginnings of Indian slavery in Virginia, at pp. 73–75. See also Carl Bridenbaugh, *Jamestown, 1544–1699* (New York: Oxford University Press, 1980).

Jesse Burt and Robert B. Ferguson: *Indians of the Southeast: Then and Now* (Nashville: Abingdon Press, 1973) attest to Tuscarora resistance to slavery.

Charles Hudson, *The Southeastern Indians* (The University of Tennessee Press, 1976), contains a full discussion of Indian slavery in the Carolinas.

John Barnwell's and James Moore's campaigns are recounted in Hugh T. Lefler and William S. Powell, *Colonial North Carolina* (New York: Charles Scribner's Sons, 1973).

I refer to Carolina as the Carolinas, even though North Carolina was not carved out of the colony until 1712. I refer to them as North and South Carolina in relating events that occurred even before they were formally divided. The settlement of Charles Town became Charleston. I have referred to it as Charleston throughout.

CHAPTER 5: INDIANS AS ALLIES: THE IROQUOIS

The author I have most relied on for a history of the Iroquois is J. R. Miller, whose recent book *Skyscrapers Touch the Heavens: A History of Indian-White Relations in Canada* (Toronto: University of Toronto Press, 1989), includes a marvellous account of the history of the Iroquois within the context of White-Native relations generally. Gary Nash's *Red, White and Black, supra,* is also very helpful on the Iroquois. I have also relied on the entry by Peter G. Ramsden entitled "Iroquois" in *The Canadian Encyclopedia,* Vol. II (Edmonton: Hurtig,

1985). I have once again found very useful D. W. Meinig's *The Shaping of America*, Vol. 1, *Atlantic America, 1492–1800*. Bruce Trigger, *Natives and Newcomers: Canada's "Heroic Age" Reconsidered*, supra, also discusses the history of the Iroquois. He summarizes the evidence on pre-contact Iroquois numbers. See also E. Palmer Patterson II, *The Canadian Indian: A History Since 1500* (Don Mills: Collier-Macmillan, 1972); Francis Jennings, *The Ambiguous Iroquois Empire* (New York: W.W. Norton, 1984); Barbara Graymont, *The Iroquois in the American Revolution* (Syracuse: Syracuse University Press, 1972).

The idea of federalism was, in 1789, an innovation in political theory. Daniel Boorstin calls it, in *The Republic of Technology* (New York: Harper & Row, 1978), "the best symbol of the Founders' spirit" (p. 57). The suggestion that the Founding Fathers borrowed from the Iroquois Confederacy is made by Bruce E. Johansen, *Forgotten Founders* (Ipswich, Mass.: Gambit, 1982), and discussed further in J. E. Chamberlin, *The Harrowing of Eden*, supra. Engels had read, and been greatly influenced by Lewis Henry Morgan, *The League of the Iroquois*, published in 1851.

Lands set aside for Indians in Canada are called Indian reserves and in the United States Indian reservations.

CHAPTER 6: JOHN MARSHALL AND THE INDIANS

The account of United States Indian policy in the formative years in Herbert Aptheker, *The Early Years of the Republic: From the End of the Revolution to the First Administration of Washington (1783–1793)* (New York: International Publishers, 1976) includes an account of the treaty ceremony with the Creeks, and a discussion of the Indian policy of the new republic.

The judgements of Chief Justice Marshall may be cited thus: *Johnson v. McIntosh*, 21 U.S. 8 Wheat 543 (1823); *Cherokee Nation v. Georgia*, 30 U.S. (5 Pet.) 1 (1831); *Worcester v. Georgia*, 31 U.S. (6 Pet.) 515 (1832); *Tee-Hit Ton v. U.S.* is cited as 348 U.S. 272 (1955).

In Russell L. Barsh and James Y. Henderson, *The Road: Indian Tribes and Political Liberty* (Berkeley and Los Angeles: University of California Press, 1980), there is a very good discussion of John Marshall's judgements. The authors say that his earlier judgement in *Cherokee Nation* has impeded the complete adoption of his more emphatic view of Indian sovereignty expressed in *Worcester*.

In G. Edward White's monumental *History of the Supreme Court of the United States* (New York and London: Macmillan, 1971) Chapter X, "Natural Law and Racial Minorities: The Court's Response to Slaves and Indians," provides an excellent account of the influence of natural law on early United States constitutional jurisprudence, and reproduces the Madison-Wirt correspondence.

The remarks by Chief Justice Brian Dickson and Mr. Justice Gerald La Forest referred to appear in *R. v. Sparrow,* (1990) D.L.R. (4th) 385.

The claims of some Native tribes on the eastern seaboard of the United States have been revived in recent years because, in certain cases, early treaties between the Indians and the states were reached in violation of the *Indian Non-Intercourse Act.*

CHAPTER 7: WARS AGAINST THE INDIANS: THE U.S. AND ARGENTINA

An excellent general history is Robert M. Utley, *The Indian Frontier of the American West, 1846–1890* (Albuquerque: University of New Mexico Press, 1984). I have also relied on Ralph K. Andrist, *The Long Death: The Last Days of the Plains Indian* (New York: Macmillan, 1964). Military aspects of the United States Indian wars are discussed in S. L. A. Marshall, *Crimsoned Prairie: The Indian Wars* (New York: Scribner, 1972). A classic account of the struggle, from the point of view of the Indians, is Alvin M. Josephy, Jr., *The Patriot Chiefs: A Chronicle of American Indian Resistance* (New York: Viking Press, 1961; rpt. ed. Penguin Books, 1976). Josephy's description of the flight of the Nez Percé is especially moving.

Accounts of the removals are found in Francis P. Preucha, *American Indian Policy in the Formative Years: Indian Trade and Intercourse Acts, 1790–1834* (Cambridge: Harvard University Press, 1962); D'Arcy McNickle, *They Came Here First: The Epic of the American Indian* (New York: Harper & Row, 1975).

Regarding President Grant and the Black Hills, I have relied on William S. McFeely, *Grant: A Biography* (New York: Norton, 1981). Indeed, as regards the Black Hills, "all difficulty in this matter" has not yet been resolved. In 1980, the Supreme Court of the United States held that the treaty forced on the Sioux by the Grant administration was illegal: *U. S. v. Sioux Nation of Indians,* 448 U.S. 371.

I have relied on Juan Carlos Walther's, *La Conquista del Desierto* (Buenos Aires: Editorial Universitorio de Buenos Aires, 1971), a military history of the Campaign of the Desert. The description of Calfucura comes from Walther, as do the quotes from Roca's speeches and the quote about hand-to-hand fighting.

I have also relied on David Rock's history, *Argentina, 1516–1987* (Berkeley and Los Angeles: University of California Press, 1987).

I enjoyed V. S. Naipaul, *The Return of Eva Perón* (New York: 1980); the quote about Argentina's "simple history" is at p. 149. Naipaul discusses Borges's attitude towards the Indians at p. 122 and p. 148.

CHAPTER 8:
RESERVES, RESERVATIONS AND REDUCCIONES

I discussed the *General Allotment Act,* 1887 and the *Alaska Native Claims Settlement Act,* 1971, in my *Village Journey, The Report of the Alaska Native Review Commission* (New York: Hill & Wang, 1985). The *General Allotment Act* was not the first of its kind. There had been allotment statutes in the United States during the 1850s, and under them a great deal of Indian land had been alienated.

For the history of the Mapuches, I have relied on Bernardo Berdichewsky, *The Araucanian Indian in Chile* (Copenhagen: I. W. G. I. A. Document Series, No. 20, 1975). I have also relied on No. 38 in the I. W. G. I. A. (International Work Group for Indigenous Affairs), Document Series entitled *Chile 1979: The Mapuche Tragedy* (Copenhagen, 1979).

I am also grateful to José Aylwin and Eduardo Castillo, for sending me their "Legislacion Sobre Indigenas en Chile a Traves de la Historia," Document No. 3, November 1990, published by the Chilean Human Rights Commission.

CHAPTER 9: GUATEMALA:
REBIRTH OF THE BLACK LEGEND

In chapters dealing with the Conquest and the settlement of the two continents I have not felt obliged to provide a lengthy list of works or sources for quotations that appear often in the history books. The events in Guatemala, however, are recent and therefore I should mention here all of the authors I have relied upon.

I found that Ronald Wright's excellent book *Time Among the Maya: Travels in Belize, Guatemala, and Mexico* (New York: Viking, 1989), gave me an understanding of what has been happening in Guatemala as good, I should think, as I am likely to obtain without visiting that country.

The quotation beginning "The people were surrounded . . . " is found at p. 220 of Wright's book and comes from Susanne Jonas, Ed McCaughan and Elizabeth Sutherland, eds., *Guatemala: Tyranny on Trial* (San Francisco: Synthesis Publications, 1984). The quotation beginning "The [soldiers] searched" is found at p. 241 of Wright's book and is from Allan Nairn, "The Guns of Guatemala: the merciless mission of Rios Montt's army," *The New Republic*, 188: 14 (1983): 17–21.

The quotation beginning "I was sitting . . . " is from Americas Watch, 1984. Americas Watch has provided the figure of one million internal refugees. The basic documents published by Americas Watch Committee are *Guatemala: A Nation of Prisoners* (Washington, 1984), and *Civil Patrols in Guatemala* (Washington, 1986). Amnesty International has published *Guatemala: The Human Rights Record* (London: Amnesty International Publications 1987). See also Julie Hodson, *Witnesses to Political Violence in Guatemala* (New York: Oxfam America, 1982).

Also important is Jim Handy, *Gift of the Devil: A History of Guatemala* (Toronto: Between the Lines Press, 1984). I have relied as well on Handy in assessing the impact of the military's campaign against the Indians. He has expressed the view that the rise of the military presents a greater threat to Indian survival than any since the Conquest itself. The figures relating to the devastation among the villages are from Handy. See also James Painter, *Guatemala: False Hope, False Freedom* (London: Catholic Institute for International Relations, 1987).

Jean-Marie Simon *Guatemala: Eternal Spring, Eternal Tyranny* (New York: Norton, 1987) discusses the savagery of the military campaign; the quotation beginning "He told me . . . " is from p. 170.

I am grateful to Steven Tullberg of the Indian Law Resource Centre in Washington, D. C., for allowing me to read his unpublished paper, written following an extensive trip he made to Guatemala in 1990. See also *The Review*, published by the International Commission of Jurists, No. 44 (June 1990), which contains a report on Guatemala.

In Edward R.F. Sheehan, *Agony in the Garden, A Stranger in Central America* (New York: Houghton Mifflin, 1989), there is a useful chapter on the events in Guatemala.

No book on the repression in Guatemala is more affecting than Rigoberta Menchú, Elizabeth Burgos, ed., Ann Wright, trans., *I, Rigoberta Menchú* (London: Verso Press, 1983).

CHAPTER 10: THE LAST REDOUBT:
THE SURVIVAL OF SUBSISTENCE

I have relied on my own *Northern Frontier, Northern Homeland: Report of the Mackenzie Valley Pipeline Inquiry,* supra, and *Village Journey: Report of the Alaska Native Review Commission,* supra.

Leading proponents of the animal rights and animal welfare movement and the anti-fur movement, together with representatives of the Native people, spoke at a conference held by Canadian Arctic Resources Committee, at McGill University, Montreal, 29–30 January 1987: ed. Robert F. Keith and Alan Saunders, *A Question of Rights, Northern Wildlife Management and the Anti-Harvest Movement* (Ottawa: Canadian Arctic Resources Committee, 1989). The statements by Thomas Coon and Stephen Best are taken from the record of the conference.

George Wenzel has written an excellent book on the same controversy: *Animal Rights, Human Rights: Ecology, Economy and Ideology in the Canadian Arctic* (Toronto: University of Toronto Press, 1991).

CHAPTER 11: NATIVE CLAIMS AND THE RULE OF LAW

I have relied on the account that I wrote of the Nisga'a case in *Fragile Freedoms* (Toronto: Clarke, Irwin, 1981). I have adapted what I wrote at that time to take account of the larger historical context and of events of the past decade.

The Nisga'a Indians case is known as *Calder v. Attorney-General of British Columbia* and is reported in (1969) 8 D. L.R. (3d) 59 (Supreme Court of British Columbia); (1970) 13 D. L. R. (3d) 64 (British Columbia Court of Appeal); and (1973) S. C. R. 313, 34 D. L. R. (3d)

145, (Supreme Court of Canada). The decision of the Supreme Court of Canada in R. v. *Sparrow* is reported in (1990) 70 D. L. R. (4th) 385.

Wilson Duff's *The Indian History of British Columbia, Vol. 1, The Impact of the White Man* (Victoria: Queen's Printer, 1965) was intended to be the first of a series, but the series was never completed, owing to Duff's untimely death. The figures for Indian populations in British Columbia are taken from Duff's book.

A recent and excellent account of White-Native relations in British Columbia is found in Paul Tennant, *Aboriginal Peoples and Politics, The Indian Land Question in British Columbia 1849–1989* (Vancouver: U.B.C. Press, 1990).

EPILOGUE

The quotation from Pablo Neruda is from *The Heights of Macchu Picchu,* supra.

The quotation from Lévi-Strauss is from Claude Lévi-Strauss, translated by John and Doreen Wightman, *Tristes Tropiques* (New York: Atheneum, 1974).

Index

Photo by Rosamond Norbury

Thomas R. Berger is a British Columbia lawyer specializing in civil liberties, constitutional law and Native rights. He is recognized internationally for his work in the areas of human rights and jurisdictional justice for the world's northern peoples. His books include *Northern Frontier, Northern Homeland, Fragile Freedoms* and *Village Journey*.